FIRST AND FASTEST

EDITED AND

FIRST AND

A COLLECTION OF ACCOUNTS OF THE WORLD'S

ILLUSTRATED WITH

HARPER & ROW, PUBLISHERS

INTRODUCED BY RICHARD HOUGH

FASTEST

GREATEST AUTO RACES

PHOTOGRAPHS AND MAPS

NEW YORK, EVANSTON, AND LONDON

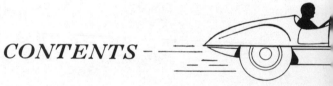

CONTENTS

ILLUSTRATIONS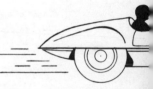

viii

EDITOR'S NOTE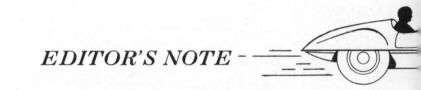

" 'Now! Now!' cried the Queen. 'Faster! Faster!' " And a little later in *Through the Looking-Glass,* Lewis Carroll has the Queen remark: "it takes all the running *you* can do to keep in the same place. If you want to get somewhere else, you must run at least twice as fast as that."

This was written some thirty years before the first auto race. But Lewis Carroll knew all about man's fundamental need to go faster than his fellows and the competitive spirit in all of us that causes records to be broken.

"Faster! Faster!" There will never be an end to it, and the auto, from the very first, provided the best means man had ever possessed for expressing his ambitions in the world of competition and record breaking. Auto racing has been with us for nearly seventy years. This book is about some of the great occasions when records were broken—when the exciting word "fastest" was on everyone's lips.

R. H.

London—1963

ACKNOWLEDGMENTS -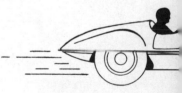

Acknowledgments are due to the following for permission
to include copyright material in this volume:

G. T. Foulis & Co. Ltd. for the chapter on the 1903
Paris–Madrid race from *Ten Years of Motors and Motor
Racing* by Charles Jarrott; the Chilton Co., publishers
of *Motor Age* magazine, for the report by Clarence Phil-
lips on the 1925 Indianapolis 500; the MG Car Co. Ltd.
for the chapter on the 1934 Tripoli Grand Prix from
Grand Prix by Barré Lyndon; the Temple Press Ltd.,

publishers of *The Motor,* for the reports on the 1937 Avusrennen and 1952 Le Mans; the Grenville Publishing Co. Ltd., publishers of *Motor Sport,* for the reports by Denis Jenkinson on the 1955 Mille Miglia and the 1958 Miglia di Monza; Time Inc., publishers of *Sports Illustrated,* for the report on the 1963 Indianapolis 500 by Kenneth Rudeen; Hutchinson & Co. Ltd. and Richard Hough for the chapter on the 1914 Tourist Trophy from *Tourist Trophy.*

FIRST AND FASTEST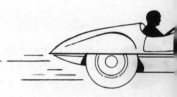

CHAPTER ONE:

Giants in the dust! The opening of the age of the automobile in Europe was heralded by a series of astonishing races, the city-to-city events that began in 1895 and reached a magnificent and disastrous climax in 1903. The cars were crude, huge, high, fast, and always critically dangerous. Herculean strength as well as courage was demanded of the driver who took these machines at speeds in the 70s and 80s over potholed roads from one European city to another. Each car trailed behind it a cloud of choking dust, and to

2

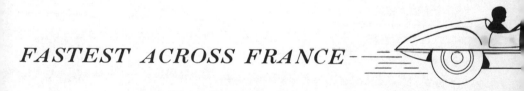

FASTEST ACROSS FRANCE--

pass another competitor on the narrow, bumpy, tree-lined
roads you had to pierce this cloud and, half-blinded and
with the other car seen as a tall, dim shape shaking along
only feet away, squeeze past with two wheels almost in the
ditch.

Most of the cars came from France or Italy—Mors,
Gobron-Brillié, Darracq, Panhard, De Dion, Peugeot,
Itala, F.I.A.T. The fame of their names rang from nation
to nation. Even better known, and admired, were the driv-

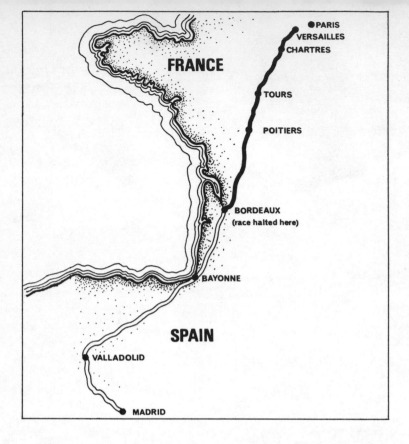

ers: giants of men like Georges Richard; Chevalier René de Knyff, who won the 1350-mile Tour de France at over 30 mph when 10 mph was considered the highest safe maximum for an automobile; Levassor of the Panhard firm, and the Renaults of the car firm of that name; Baron de Crawhez; the Italian mountain of muscle Lancia; the great Jenatzy; George Heath from America, the first of so many of his fellow countrymen who were to flock to Europe half a century later to fight for the champion's laurels; and Earp, Edge, and Jarrott from Britain.

The last named of these British drivers wrote the following graphic account of the Paris-Madrid race of 1903,

4

an event that saw higher speeds, closer competition, and greater heroism than any previous city-to-city race. It also saw greater excitement among the crowds than ever before.

No wonder the people came out to cheer, all the way from the starting point at Versailles just outside Paris! And they also were the cause of the abandonment of these races, for their enthusiasm was often beyond control, and over the hundreds of miles of road there were never enough police or soldiers to hold them back. It was one thing for drivers and their mechanics to be killed, quite another for young, overexcited boys and other innocent bystanders to be hurled to their deaths by the passing monsters. The city-to-city races finally succumbed to their own success. But while they lasted they must have been one of the great sights of Europe.

THE CHIEF CONTESTANTS	
DRIVERS	**CARS**
Marcel Renault (France)	Renault (France)
Lorraine Barrow (Britain)	De Dietrich (France)
R. Stead (Britain)	De Dietrich (France)
Charles Jarrott (Britain)	De Dietrich (France)
Camille Jenatzy (France)	Mercedes (Germany)
Louis Renault (France)	Renault (France)
M. Gabriel (France)	Mors (France)
M. Salleron (France)	Mors (France)

BY CHARLES JARROTT

Paris-Bordeaux! The very name conjures up old memories of struggles, grim and fierce, and thrilling fights among those whose names are now almost forgotten, but who, on the old Paris-Bordeaux road, struggled on bicycles in years past for the title of "King of the Road."

It all began in the days before motors were thought of, and when the motorcycle held its own as the most rapid form of road vehicle. Mills, Holbein, Huret, Lesna, Linton —great riders of their day—struggled hard to win the great road race of the year, Paris-to-Bordeaux. Later, De Knyff, Charron, Girardot, Farman, Fournier, and others whose names are quite forgotten fought the same battles over the same long straight stretches. Their course was fleet and the pace was fierce, but it was all on the same old fascinating road; and as a grand finale Paris to Bordeaux was the first and, as it eventually turned out, the last stage of the last great inter-country race from Paris to Madrid.

What do I remember of that race?

Long avenues of trees, top-heavy with foliage, and gaunt in their very nakedness of trunk; a long, never-ending white ribbon, stretching away to the horizon; the holding of a bullet directed to that spot on the skyline where earth and heaven met; fleeting glimpses of towns and dense masses of people—mad people, insane and reckless, holding themselves in front of the bullet to be ploughed and cut and maimed to extinction, evading the inevitable at the last moment in frantic haste; overpowering relief, as each mass was passed and each chance of catastrophe escaped; and beyond all, a horrible feeling of being hunted. Hundreds of cars behind, of all sizes and powers, and all of them at my heels, traveling over the same road, perhaps faster than I, and all striving to overtake me, pour dust over me, and leave me behind as they sped on to the distant goal of Bordeaux.

Even at the start the remembrance of the gigantic line of vehicles at Versailles, all waiting to receive the signal to dash after me, weighed me down, and as we sped on and they came not, the strain became worse and worse. I have sympathy now with the hunted animal; for once in my life I was hunted. And of all the impressions of that wild rush to Bordeaux that awful feeling of being hunted was the most vivid and lasting. Having experienced it, I do not wonder that No. 1* has seldom won a race.

Then came that long lapse at Bordeaux after my arrival, and the ominous rumors which trickled through as the cars began to arrive. Stories of death and fearful accidents, drivers killed and spectators maimed. Along with the confirmation of these rumors came the realization that the inevitable had at last happened—that the last chapter had been written of the great sport, and that inter-country races could be held no more. There was the longing for news of friends in the race; anxiety at their nonarrival; grief at the realization that of the many sufferers, one of my best friends was terribly injured! I live it all over again, and I think it impossible for anyone to have gone through in one day more varied sensations than I experienced on that eventful day when we started from Paris to go to Bordeaux.

Hundreds of cars of all sorts, shapes, and sizes. Some

* The first driver to leave the line at the staggered start.

unsafe, unsuitable, and impossible. Some driven by men with every qualification as drivers of racing cars; others with drivers having no qualifications—all let loose over that long, broad Bordeaux road.

I went back over the road after the race and I marveled, not that several had been killed, but that so many had escaped. Cars in fragments, cars in fields, some upside down, others with no wheels. The sufferers were not all inexperienced; and two of the old brigade, Marcel Renault and Lorraine Barrow, handled the steering wheel for the last time, drove their last race and paid the extreme penalty.

The "Race to Death"! It need not have been so, but by an unfortunate combination of circumstances the leveling up of the penalties payable for the risk of motor racing took place in one event. Before and since, what escapes many drivers have had! The same terrible smashes were experienced, but no penalty was exacted.

My old love had been forsaken. For the first time I was discarding the Panhard for the De Dietrich. Since my previous victory in the Circuit des Ardennes I had started my own business in London, and selected the De Dietrich firm as the most progressive of all the French manufacturers. I hoisted their colors and accepted the leading position in their team for the Paris-Madrid race in the year 1903.

De Dietrich et Cie had in the years gone by occupied a prominent position in the French industry, and the racing cars they were building for the Paris-Madrid race were not the first vehicles of the kind made by them. The brains of Turcat and Mery, the well-known French engineers, had, however, been brought to the assistance of the De Dietrich house, and although the racing program was not new, the cars themselves were of a power and type entirely novel. And I, as driver of one of these cars, had to stand or fall by its capabilities and behavior in the actual race.

Peculiarly enough, the three big cars made by Messrs. De Dietrich for the race were all to be driven by Englishmen: Stead, a sturdy Yorkshireman, acclimatized to France by many years of residence, one of the very oldest of the old racing crowd; Lorraine Barrow, an Englishman resident at Biarritz, and one of the experts of the Continent; and myself. De Dietrich cars of smaller power were being driven by several other drivers, including the famous woman driver Madame du Gast, but the real hope of De Dietrich lay in one of the three big cars.

I have already explained that the racing cars were of a new type, and I realized this when for one long, long week before the start I watched my car being built and rebuilt. The first trouble that happened was that through a miscalculation the car was considerably over the 1,000-kilo limit. Everything was done to bring the weight down, but unsuccessfully, and at the last moment an engine of considerably less horsepower had to be fitted. I may say that this new engine had been put through as a safeguard in the event of the car weighing too heavy. The additional advantages obtained here, however, were that much stronger axles and much stronger springs were fitted, as the weight saved through the use of a smaller motor was very considerable, and we decided that in view of the bad roads of Spain it might be a better policy to build the carriage to stand the fearful roads it would have to travel over in Spain than to construct it merely with a view to speed.

Innumerable troubles presented themselves one after

the other, and we almost despaired that the car would be ready in time for the race. As for its being properly tried prior to the start, this was an absolute impossibility. My one great consolation lay in the fact that Stead's and Barrow's machines were giving as much, or nearly as much, trouble as mine.

Barrow and I lived together, worked together, and waited together during that wretched week in Paris, when it seemed impossible for human hands to overcome the troubles which cropped up at every turn in preparing our cars. However, by a desperate effort the cars were ready in time for the weighing-in preliminaries before the race, and having carried out the requirements in regard to weight by stripping the cars to the very last ounce, we returned to the garage to have them pulled down again and further alterations made.

The lighter-powered cars were all right, and as they left the garage one by one on the day before the start, we three unlucky Englishmen bemoaned our fate and agreed that Madrid would never see us. Then Stead got away with his car, off to Versailles, where we were staying overnight, ready for the start in the morning. Then Barrow's car was ready, and he shook hands and said he would keep dinner for me; and I was left disconsolate, realizing that even if my car went at all, I had no chance of doing anything with it, as I had never had it on the road.

Seven o'clock in the evening, and at last all was ready. The slipping clutch, which had been giving all the trouble, had been arranged with a long lever to which a strap was attached, and I was informed that if I had trouble with my clutch I was to hang on to the strap and force it to hold. How I was to do this and drive a racing car at eighty miles

10

an hour at the same time was not explained. However, the mechanics had been working on my car for three nights running, with the keenest possible enthusiasm, and for their sakes I determined at least to start and see how far I could get before disaster overtook me.

So off I dashed to Versailles to food and sleep, and to the last preparations for the race on the morrow.

No. 1 was to be my starting position on the following morning, and as I slipped over the ground out of Paris I thought that an appropriate place for me would have been at the end instead of the beginning of the procession. To my astonishment, however, the car was going well. Untried as it was, I nevertheless quickly realized that it was capable of traveling quite fast; but as for Madrid, why of course it was an impossibility, and this knowledge made my expression very gloomy as I walked into the Hotel des Reservoirs at Versailles on my arrival.

Barrow had been true to his word and had held up dinner as long as possible. But by the time I arrived he had given it up, and he and Stead had settled down for their last good meal before arrival in Bordeaux on the following day. Then occurred one of those tragic little prophecies which are met with sometimes through that strange law which seems in some manner to give an inkling to mankind of the dark and misty future. The incident is as clearly defined in my memory now as when it occurred. As I approached, Barrow was raising a glass to his lips, and seeing me walking toward him, he set it down and expressed his delight that I had at last got to the start safely. Then seeing me still lugubrious and unhappy, he slapped me on the back, and again raising his glass, exclaimed: "Whatever is the matter with you? Are we not all here? Let us eat, drink, and be merry, for tomorrow we die!"—words spoken in jest, but fulfilled to the bitter end. On the morrow, when it was rumored that my companions of the previous evening were among the dead left on the road, the scene and words came back to me with horrible distinctness.

At two o'clock on the following morning Barrow came into my bedroom and roused me from a very sound slumber. If I had considered that I had a chance at all of doing reasonably well, I should have been willing and eager to be up getting ready. But as it was I was very cross and fractious, for I thought that in all probability the result of my efforts would be that I should hopelessly break down within ten kilometers of the start. However, Barrow had me up, and after a hurried cup of chocolate we were both out in the darkness getting our cars to make our way to the start.

For some inexplicable cause my car, which had taken an hour to start on the previous evening, started up immediately. Perhaps Bianchi, who was my mechanic and was accompanying me for the first time in a big race, had during the night coaxed it into a submissive mood. But try as we would, Barrow's car would not start. Eventually, with a shake of the hand, I had to leave him to his task, as, being first, I had to be in my position early.

Never did I wish a friend good luck more sincerely than I did Lorraine Barrow on that eventful morning, and never did a wish go more awry. It was the last time I ever saw him, and the memory of that hand grip in the darkness in the hotel yard at Versailles is one of my few sad recollections in connection with motor racing.

Picking my way carefully through the thousands of sightseers in Versailles, I arrived at the park from which the start was to take place and got to the front of the long line already formed. The thousands assembled to see the start had availed themselves of every possible point of vantage, and a dense living mass filled the road right through the park. The raising of the curtain on the last great act of road racing of the old style was dramatic and inspiring, with a vast concourse assembled to witness it, and unhappy as I was when I considered my own chance of winning the race, it was nevertheless a thrilling moment when I took my place, the very first car to start, with hundreds to follow me to Madrid.

De Knyff was No. 2 and Louis Renault No. 3. Those of us in front decided that it was too dark at 3:30—the time fixed for the start—and so a respite of a further fifteen minutes was granted before dispatching me.

I asked what would happen to the swaying mass of people blocking the road when I started, and the only answer I received was a shrug of the shoulders and a reply that they could clear soon enough when I once got going. The soldiers intended for keeping the course clear were swallowed up in the huge concourse of spectators, and disorder reigned supreme.

Three forty-five at last. On with the switch and away went the motor. A hundred handshakes and a mighty roar from the crowd, and I was off. It seemed impossible that my swaying, bounding car could miss the reckless spectators. A wedge-shaped space opened out in the crowd as I approached, and so fine was the calculation made that at times it seemed impossible for the car not to overtake the apex of the human triangle and deal death and destruction. I tried slowing down, but quickly realized that the danger was as great at forty miles an hour as at eighty. It

13

merely meant that the crowd waited a longer time in the road; and the remembrance of those hundreds of cars behind me and the realization that the hunt had commenced made me put on top speed and hope that Providence would be kind to the weak intellects which allowed their possessors to run such risks so callously.

Regarding that portion of the Paris-Bordeaux road to Chartres, I was ignorant. After Chartres I remembered it well, but the first corner after leaving the park at Versailles nearly led to my undoing. As a matter of instinct in motor racing, when traveling over a strange road and being in doubt as to the direction, one always took the road on which most people happened to be congregated; and on this occasion, coming to a fork, I decided to take the road to the right, when suddenly, as I arrived at the corner, I perceived the left-hand road was the correct one. Although traveling at eighty miles an hour, I saw that I could just make the turn, and as we swung around we missed the curbstone by inches.

I previously mentioned that my engine had had no running on the road, and now as I began to press her she began to clank in an ominous manner. It was obvious that she required very gentle handling, and I slackened a little while Bianchi slaved at the lubricating pump and poured oil into the base chamber.

My great trouble was with my clutch, which persisted in slipping. I had, however, the long metal lever and strap, and by pulling on the strap we could do what the clutch spring refused to do, namely, make the clutch hold. Until Bianchi had to start pumping oil, he of course hung on to the strap and prevented the clutch slipping, but he required two hands to pump, and even then it was terribly hard work. Hence I had to hold on to the strap with one hand and steer with the other. And still we were pegging away on to Rambouillet and Chartres.

It was not unexpected, however, when before Rambouillet was reached Bianchi by gesticulation told me that De Knyff was just behind. We must have been traveling well in spite of my having reduced speed, for it took him some considerable time before he got by and dropped us. And then Louis Renault came along very fast and was soon away. Immediately afterward we reached Rambouillet control and found both cars there. De Knyff, however, was in trouble with his ignition, and he being delayed, I followed Renault out of the control. Soon after De Knyff came along again, but stopped immediately, and this was the last time I saw him.

Renault was traveling magnificently, but we also were going well, and I had hopes that I should pull back the lead he had gained. I was delighted with the way my De Dietrich was behaving. Practically its first trial on the road, and it was running like an old, well-tried car. And then suddenly, with a sob, the motor stopped. If there was one particular trouble in racing from which I suffered most it was stoppages in the fuel pipe, and this was the cause of my stoppage on this occasion. As I drew up on the grass at the right-hand side of the road, I wondered how many cars would pass me before I got going again. We quickly located the trouble and started to disconnect the pipe from the tank and carburetor to clear it. The sensation I have mentioned of being hunted had overpowered me from the very start, and as we worked away it was almost with a sense of relief that I expected the other cars to come up and thus enable me to join in the chase instead of being chased myself. It was a glorious morning, not then six o'clock, the sun shining and the air so clear and fresh; and after the roar and rush of the wind when the car had been traveling, everything seemed so still. Not a sound could be heard except our own labored breathing as we toiled on at the car. In vain I listened for the well-known hum in the distance, betokening the approach of another car. It seemed incredible. We appeared to have stopped hours and yet no cars had overtaken us. Where was De Knyff? Where were the 90-hp Mercedes which were to have overwhelmed us at the very start? Where were the big Panhards? Had some terrible catastrophe happened and the road become blocked in some manner or other? It seemed impossible that we could have traveled at a speed sufficient to have gained so much time on all the rest.

And then we finished our work, the motor started up, Bianchi resumed his pumping, and we were off again en route for Tours. It was almost with a sickening feeling that I realized I was still the goal which the struggling multitude behind were endeavoring to overtake. As a race of sheer enjoyment I only appreciated that portion after Tours. The worries of the engine and the clutch, and the dense masses of people at every town, made the experience anything but pleasurable, keen as I was on the sport. In addition to this, in every control I was by myself. I might have been endeavoring to create a great record entirely alone instead of being one of hundreds of cars rushing to Bordeaux, for I saw none of them. Louis Renault was in front, but so far in front that he had left each control before I arrived.

And then, just before Tours, Werner in one of the huge Mercedes racers came along, and after a tussle got by, and at last I had company. We had done so well that the fact that no other cars had caught us pleased me beyond measure, and as we trundled through Tours to the outward control, little Bianchi's face, greasy and oily, was one broad grin of approval; and whether I was having a good time or not, it was perfectly clear that he was glorying in his first experience of a big road-race. Never was any engineer keener over his engines than Bianchi was over any car which I was driving in a race, and even his lack of knowledge of the French language did not prevent his capturing from under the noses of the guardian mechanics on the road—whether they belonged to De Dietrich or not—all and everything necessary for the good running and health of the car. I think his unadulterated enjoyment had something to do with the sheer abandon with which I drove the remainder of the race to Bordeaux. On going back over the times I find that all my time was lost over that first half of the journey, and that from Tours on, our times were not touched by any other competitor.

While we waited at the outward control at Tours another car rolled up, and I was delighted to find that it was Stead in his De Dietrich, starting No. 5. Halfway to Bordeaux, and out of the first four cars two were Dietrich—this seemed a good record for the *marque*. However, for some reason or other, Stead was very gloomy. He grumbled at his car and abused his mechanics for some fault or another in a splendid combination of English and French. I inquired for news of Lorraine Barrow and learned that he had arrived at the start all right, and moreover Stead had seen him at a control some distance back, when he was going very well. In the middle of my conversation with Stead Werner's time expired and he was dispatched, and a gasp

17

went out from the crowd as they saw the manner in which his car rushed up the winding road out of Tours. One minute after, I was off and soon into his dust. Five kilometers farther on, with a wrench of the wheel I just missed the fragments of his car in the road, smashed to bits, and in the same second I saw both Werner and his man standing by the car, obviously unhurt, and the former sufficiently unconcerned as to be occupied in lighting a cigarette even before he could have known the cause of the accident. It appeared that his back axle had broken when traveling at top speed and his escape must have been miraculous; but nothing could shake the calm characteristic not only of the Fatherland but also of most of the best drivers of racing cars. It does not do to have nerves if engaged in driving a racing car, but Werner's stolidity was out of the ordinary, and his smash occurred so suddenly that he could have had no warning.

Louis Renault was thirty-five minutes ahead, but we were now utilizing the full power of the motor, and the car was traveling grandly. Corners did not exist. Hills disappeared, and on the long straight stretches it was merely a question of holding on.

Ruffec at last, and here we were in trouble. More delay in the changing of an ignition plate, red-hot from the heat of the engine. How long it took us I know not. I remember a blazing-hot sun, a crowd of spectators who crowded on us regardless of our warnings that other cars were coming along the road, and the handling of red-hot pieces of metal with our bare hands, not noticing, in our feverish haste to be off again, that every time we took hold of these fiery parts the touch blistered white and hot. A welcome glass of champagne, and we were off and away once more to Angoulême.

Talking of champagne reminds me of the manner and method of taking food on these road events. Of course it was possible in the controls to obtain almost anything in the way of refreshments. I seldom arrived in a town without finding a friend ready with some form of food and drink, but the difficulty was that if trouble was being experienced it was seldom possible either to eat or drink. I remember seeing Bianchi, suddenly attacked with hunger, munching a roll of bread which had received in some unhappy manner a bath of lubricating oil; but, as he explained to me afterward, so intent was he on our engine that he had not noticed what he was eating.

Faster and still faster, until we seemed to be merely skimming over the ground, and a savage joy possessed me when I realized that we were holding our own with the hunters. The game was probably escaping; anyhow we had not been caught. The reckless crowds, assembled in the road at the entrance to each village and town, now held no terror. We slackened for nothing. Bordeaux 120 kilometers away, and we had not been caught and overwhelmed by that long line I had seen as I made my way to the start in the morning. Renault was in front, but he was not in our class, and we were now gaining even on him. Then away in the distance, on the hill, Angoulême came in sight, and another stage had been completed.

Here the inhabitants and spectators were frantic with excitement and congratulations; flowers and fruit were showered upon us. Then an excited official at the control rushed up and said that Jenatzy, in a 90 Mercedes, had left the last control and was hard on my heels, and he implored me for the sake of *la belle France* to beat the German car into Bordeaux. And I rose to the occasion and swore that come what may my De Dietrich would finish first before any German car should be allowed to enter Bordeaux. I was also informed that Renault was still thirty-five minutes ahead, so that any hope of beating him was gone unless he broke down before Bordeaux.

Just as we were off, Bianchi got down and gave a hurried look around the car to see if everything was all right for our last dash, and suddenly he informed me with horror in his voice that our front wheels were coming to pieces, the spokes having loosened themselves in the hub. I think I should have got down and investigated the matter had it not been for the knowledge that Jenatzy was coming on just behind me and might arrive at any moment. The bystanders saw the trouble also and were terribly excited when I told Bianchi to jump in. If the wheels held up, a bucket of water thrown on each at Bordeaux—to make the wood expand and fit tighter—would put them right for the next stage, but we had to get to Bordeaux, and I could do nothing but take the risk.

The road after Angoulême is a series of twists and turns, corners and angles, and it was on this portion of the road that most of the unfortunate accidents in the race took place. It was here, however, that we made our biggest gain. At this stage I was driving as for my life, Jenatzy behind, Renault in front, and as corner after corner was negotiated, and nearer and nearer we drew to the finish, with my car going better than ever, I longed for another two hundred kilometers in which to make up our lost time before Tours. That our wheels might go at any moment had not entered my head after leaving Angoulême, and when suddenly in the distance a white flag stretched across the road appeared, it almost seemed incredible that we had covered the ninety kilometers between Angoulême and Bor-

20

Charles Jarrott draws in at Bordeaux in his De Dietrich.

deaux so quickly. We averaged over sixty miles an hour over this stretch, and gained twenty minutes on Louis Renault, finishing fifteen minutes after him.

No one had expected that there was any possibility of my finishing in almost the same position as that in which I had started, but it is the unexpected which always happens in racing, and the De Dietrich car, regarding which little had been said prior to the event, had provided a sensation of the race.

I was surprised to see so many friends at the control in Bordeaux. English and French, they impressed upon me their gratification and satisfaction at my having got through so successfully. Then, with an official on my car, I made my way into the town to the closed park, where the cars were locked up until the start on the second stage.

A long interval took place before any other cars arrived. I made my way to my hotel and afterward back to the control to watch other arrivals. One or two cars arrived, but very little information was forthcoming from their drivers; they all seemed very vague as to what had happened to any cars other than their own.

Then in some extraordinary manner it began to be whispered that terrible accidents had happened, but no one knew from whence these rumors had come, only everybody was uneasy and fearful. Presently the cars began to roll in thick and fast, and the rumors were confirmed by the various drivers, but instead of being accurate in detail, everything was exaggerated. Every driver had a different story, until at last it seemed as if the road must have been bestrewn with dead and dying. Who was killed? Who was hurt? What had happened? A feeling of horror came over those of us assembled in the control that we were participating in a great carnage, and the lack of reliable information made matters so much worse.

Charron eventually arrived, having driven a touring car in the race with ladies as passengers, as he had not been able to get his racing car in time, and from him I learned more than from anyone else. There had undoubtedly been some terrible accidents, and I was horrified to learn that Lorraine Barrow and Stead in their De Dietrichs were smashed up and seriously injured and not expected to live, Barrow's mechanic having been killed on the spot. Stead had been cut down by another car and had capsized at eighty miles an hour. Barrow had struck a dog, deranged his steering, and struck a tree head-on at top speed. Marcel Renault had also smashed and there had been dozens of

*Typical sights, after the race,
on the wreckage-strewn road to Bordeaux.
These cars are Barrow's (ABOVE) and
Stead's De Dietrichs.*

other accidents en route. Charron said he had never seen anything like the scene the road presented.

Other cars came in and other stories were told. An English car driven by a novice had upset on a corner, and the unfortunate Englishman accompanying the driver had been pinned under the car, which caught fire and burned him to death. In Chatellerault a child had dashed in front of one of the cars and a soldier had rushed to save it. The driver, endeavoring to avoid both, not only struck and killed them, but also dashed into the crowd.

I need not recapitulate the list of deaths. The English papers of May 25 had the details of what they termed the "Race to Death."

Road racing was dead. Never again would it be possible to suggest a speed event over the open roads, and the sport—which, while it was sport, was in my opinion the best of all sports—was finished. The peculiar thing about it all was that the outside world had not appreciated up to that moment that there was an element of danger in motor racing. One or two drivers had certainly been injured, but accidents were very rare; and then suddenly, by one of those compensations which occur with all things in life, the toll was paid in one event, and so heavy was it that with a shudder and a gasp the world at large realized that motor racing might be really deadly.

Bordeaux that night was filled with an anxious, terrified crowd. Some of the drivers were unnerved after what had taken place, and the great topic was what had really happened on the road and whether the race ought to be stopped.

Louis Renault's joy at achieving the magnificent performance of having arrived first and winning his class (although his was not the fastest time) was turned to sorrow and grief, and he left Bordeaux that night to attend the death-bed of his brother Marcel. News came in that Stead and Barrow were both in the same hospital at Libourne, both at death's door. And much as I wanted to go on to Madrid, there would have been no satisfaction in winning a race under such unhappy circumstances.

The French Government decided the matter for everybody concerned. The race was stopped forthwith and all the racing cars taken possession of by the authorities. Special trains were secured, and the cars were dragged to the railway station behind horses and returned to Paris; not even the motors were allowed to be started.

The fastest time from Paris to Bordeaux was accomplished by Gabriel in his Mors car, and as an extraordinary piece of driving it stands unequaled and will always stand alone. Starting 168th, he came right through the scores of cars, blinding dust clouds, and wrecks in 5 hr. 14 min. running time, averaging over 65 mph. Salleron, in another Mors, finished second in 5 hr. 47 min.; and I was classified third, covering the 557 kilometers in 5 hr. 52 min.

Two days later I went back over the road in a touring car, accompanied by Baron de Turckheim and Madame du Gast, who had driven so splendidly in the race itself, and who had stayed and rendered first aid to Stead when she had come upon him immediately after his smash.

The number of cars left upon the road was extraordinary. Whether the dust or the winding nature of the road was the cause, I cannot say, but we came upon car after car abandoned from one cause or another. A driver of a light De Dietrich had taken one corner too fast, and the car was absolutely upside down on a heap of stones. The driver and mechanic were Englishmen. The peasants nearby informed us that after the smash—in which neither of the occupants of the car was hurt—the first thing the amateur mechanic did was to rescue his camera from the car and take a snapshot of it. Farther on we came on the spot where Mayhew, who had driven well, had run off the road in his Napier through the steering breaking, and had had a miraculous escape from death. Stead's car, still upside down, was inspected, and we were able to see clearly marked on the front wheel where the other car had cut him down as it passed. Most of the other cars were smashed to pieces, and I think the only thing that saved Stead was the fact that he capsized in a ditch and the car formed a sort of bridge over his body; otherwise, only immediate death

could have resulted. The most fearsome and terrible sight, however, was the fragments which remained of Lorraine Barrow's car. It appeared that when traveling at top speed —about eighty miles an hour—he had struck a dog which had been allowed to stray into the road, and this jammed his steering gear. In a flash he struck, head-on, a huge tree. His mechanic, Pierre, a Spaniard and an old servant of Barrow's, was shot out of the car straight into the tree, which he struck with his head, and was killed on the spot. Barrow himself was flung out of the car, clearing the tree and pitching over twenty yards away into the ditch on the side of the road, sustaining terrible and, as it eventually proved, fatal injuries.

I have in many races seen many cars wrecked from

The winner, M. Gabriel,
arriving at Bordeaux in his Mors.

one cause or another, but never could I have conceived it possible for any car to be so completely broken up as was Barrow's. One of the front spring hangers was driven up to the hilt and broken off short in the tree, the force of the impact having been so great that the strap holding up the starting handle and the string and leaden customs seal were also driven right into the solid wood. The car, as a car, did not exist. The shock had torn the motor out of the frame and hurled it yards away, and even the pistons in the motor were in fragments; frame, gearbox, and road wheels were all in small pieces. As I stood and gazed on the ghastly evidence of this tragedy I thought how quickly had come the end to my cheery and good-natured friend. At one moment slipping along on the road, all well, driving a fine race and rejoicing in the knowledge that Bordeaux was but thirty kilometers away, and then the fearful crash, the momentary realization of disaster, oblivion, and eventually—death.

And thus ended the most dramatic race in the history of automobilism. Dramatic, because of its surprising incidents, of Gabriel's marvelous drive, and of the coloring which is always given to an event which provides a tragedy. It was the last great road-race ever to be run on the classic French roads. I say the last, because I do not put circuit racing in the same category as those straight-away races from one place to another. Paris-Amsterdam, Paris-Berlin, Paris-Vienna—all were of the past, never to be repeated; and to my mind it was a fitting end to an inevitable happening that the curtain should have been rung down on the Paris-Bordeaux road, the scene of many a great race and titanic struggle, and the road on which Levassor himself showed to the world at large, in the first great motor race in history, the vast and far-reaching possibilities of the motor-propelled vehicle.

PARIS–MADRID 1903 RESULTS		
1ST	M. Gabriel	Mors 65.3 mph average
2ND	M. Salleron	Mors
3RD	Charles Jarrott	De Dietrich

CHAPTER TWO:

In the early years of this century a series of motor races was held on Long Island near New York. The sponsor, organizer, and donor of the cup to bear his name was the multimillionaire William K. Vanderbilt, Jr.—"An enthusiast extraordinary, a rough and ready sportsman . . . a man of convictions and a man of action," as one contemporary reporter described him; "a slight, boyish figure, alive in every nerve and muscle, alert in every brain cell, cheerful and confident in every facial line."

30

FASTEST ON LONG ISLAND

*Before opening the first of the early Vanderbilt Cup
races in 1904, Vanderbilt said, "We Americans have, I believe, some fallacious ideas with regard to racing. With
many of us the straightaway course seems the acme of ex-
cellence. To start a car at top speed on a perfectly level,
perfectly easy course and to let it go until it stops from
sheer weariness of motor or driver—that is not racing. The
personal element is the essential element. Judgment, skill,
endurance, knowledge of your car—these things are what*

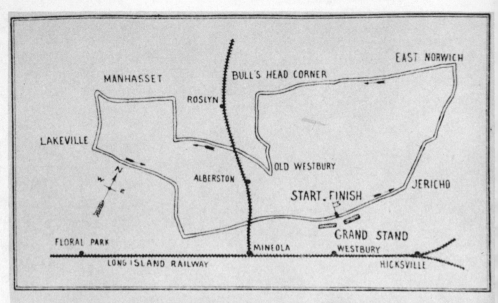

SKETCH MAP OF THE COURSE.

make winners. Such a course is the Long Island circuit. It is a course where the race will be won by the best driver, not the fastest car. I do not mean that a fast car is not a requisite to success, but I believe greatly in the value of the man behind the steering wheel."

And what of this course of Vanderbilt's? It was a thirty-mile circuit in the form of a right-angled triangle. "The hypotenuse from Queens to Jericho," wrote a correspondent who traversed the course in a "Gray Wolf" Packard, "is the best section of the road. From Jericho to Beth Page road, a distance of about six miles, is fair to middling. From Beth Page, where the turning is at right angles, the road for five or six miles is as bad as can be. After that it widens and is fairly decent to the apex of the triangle at

32

Queens." The same reporter wrote of the railroad crossing on the Jericho turnpike: "The encounter is not pleasant, especially when one learns by inquiring among the gatemen and railroad employees that they had heard nothing so far of any precautions against accidents in the way of shutting off traffic during the race. This is not encouraging . . . For a mile or two further along this road the number of hummocks is altogether too abundant for comfort. Some of them are not ordinary ruts but good wide holes 5 or 6 feet across, and anywhere from 4 inches to 1 foot deep. These will take a lot of fixing unless the race is to be an affair of flying through the air. At New Hyde Park, a straggling village on one side of the turnpike, I found the residents very enthusiastic over the prospective speed carnival. Their enthusiasm was not lessened by the fact that at this point the private road leading to Mr. Vanderbilt's country house at Great Neck branches off from the highway. The young patron of the great road race is very popular hereabouts, and country bumpkins are proud to point out his residence. . . ."

It was to the great satisfaction of Vanderbilt, Jr. that the first of his races was won by a fellow countryman who had already had great success in Europe, George Heath, driving a 90-hp Panhard. Albert Clement, a Frenchman driving one of his own cars was second. The race was spoiled by hooligans who attempted to halt the cars with nails on the road and, incidentally, killed or injured several drivers and mechanics as a result, and by the crowds who poured onto the roads after the first three competitors passed the post.

Two comments on that first event are worth noting. The first is that of Vanderbilt himself. "Looking back after

33

a strenuous week, I think we can all congratulate ourselves upon the success of the first American road race. It was a good, clean contest, full of interest, and I think the people who took part in it, as well as the public, are on the whole perfectly satisfied that everything was done which could be done to make it a success." Winner Heath was less content. "I cannot say that the race was at all certain when I started," he commented. "I merely started out to do my best, and was much put out because unable to give my car its full speed. This course is a beautiful one for a speed of 30 mph, but at twice that speed there are irregularities that seem terrible. . . . " So much for the roads!

| THE CHIEF CONTESTANTS ||
DRIVERS	CARS
L. Wagner (Germany)	Darracq (France)
V. Lancia (Italy)	F.I.A.T. (Italy)
C. Jenatzy (France)	Mercedes (Germany)
F. Nazzaro (Italy)	F.I.A.T. (Italy)
A. Duray (France)	Lorraine-Dietrich (France)

The third and final, and fastest of the Vanderbilt Cup Races, in their early series, was run on the same course, though in much improved form, on October 8, 1906. It again drew many of the great European drivers and cars and turned into an exciting duel between Louis Wagner of Germany, in a 120-hp Darracq, Vincenzo Lancia of Italy, in a F.I.A.T. of similar power, and the great Camille Jenatzy, in a Mercedes.

The speed of the race this year went up from some 30 mph to 61.43 mph. "The drivers were hindered from making faster time by the mad public which crowded the circuit," wrote the American correspondent of Lord Montagu's magazine *The Car Illustrated*, who continued:

"One fatality occurred when Elliott F. Shepard's Hotchkiss, the highest-powered car in the contest, struck Curt L. Grueber at King's Corner and instantly killed him. Two boys were hurt, one by Tracy (Locomobile), and another by Dr. Weilschott (F.I.A.T.). It is remarkable that many more were not seriously injured, considering the reckless manner in which thousands of people stayed until the last minute directly in the path of the oncoming motors."

A thousand deputy sheriffs were not enough to keep the 300,000 spectators under control. But despite the unfortunate transgression of the multitude upon the rights of the course, which greatly retarded the speed of the cars, the race is considered the greatest of its kind by both foreign and American drivers. Out of eighteen entries there

35

was but one withdrawal at the eleventh hour, that of Foxhall Keene's Mercedes. . . . Two drivers withdrew from the race after starting: one of these was Weilschott, who broke the steering gear on the first round, and the other, Shepard, who withdrew when he learned that his car had caused the death of a spectator.

"To the American eye," *The Car Illustrated* reporter continued, "the spectacle with all its attending circumstances far surpassed any record of the great feats of skill of the ancient Grecian or Roman amphitheater. The first spectators began steadily to arrive in the neighborhood of the course the day before the race and continued to come all through the day and night until the bomb, announcing the start, had exploded. People who did not know a steam car from an electric vehicle were caught in the dragnet of the prevailing excitement and went to experience a new sensation—a sensation to make of them, no matter what their nocturnal discomfort, confirmed Vanderbilters and followers of the car.

"The race did not start until 6 A.M., but all night long the cars came down to Jericho Turnpike from the city, passing King's Corner with horns, chimes, and sirens sounding their different notes. Touring cars, limousines, runabouts, sometimes three, sometimes four abreast on the wide roadway; wheel to wheel and hub to hub they came, myriad lights of gas, electricity, and oil startling the night. On account of the fog that hung over the upper part of the circuit, the start was delayed fifteen minutes. At 6:15 Le Blon, whose unprecedented overconfidence has cost him many a race, shot over the tape, and Heath's Panhard was driven to the line. After a minute had elapsed he was gone with a slow start.

Jenatzy's Mercedes swings through East Norwich.

"Jenatzy, the excitable, worried over a little trouble and getting the car exactly on the mark. The starter began to count the last seconds backward in French. On *cinq*, Jenatzy adjusted his goggles. On *Partez!* he raised his hand in salute, slipped in the clutch, and started easily.

"Lancia, in his F.I.A.T., the left side exhausts vomiting white flame, came up cool and smiling *sans* his erstwhile mustache. As he crossed the tape he raised both hands to adjust his goggles, then, quickly gaining headway, disappeared.

"Lawell (America), in the peculiar air-cooled Frayer-Miller, shakes hands with the owner of the car and starts with cool calculation.

"Shepard with a fresh cigarette between his lips,

Duray's Lorraine-Dietrich, which placed third

which he throws away when the last seconds commence, seems happy that he is starting another big race. He advances his spark control halfway around the semicircle before he slips in the clutch, and then, saluting with his right hand, is off, the Hotchkiss roaring mightily.

"Luttgen, driving Brown's Mercedes, is hidden by clouds of oil smoke as he comes to the mark, and as he departs a trail of fire issues from the exhaust.

"Nazzaro and his tiny mechanic wear ordinary golfing caps and small goggles. The F.I.A.T. gets away slowly, but the Italian driver is unmoved.

"There were many cheers for the American, Tracy, in the Locomobile that differed but little from the car which he drove to third place the year before. He was smil-

Wagner takes the checkered flag.

ing, with a gentlemanly poise of the head, and had an extra pair of goggles around his neck.

"Wagner and Vivet, his mechanic, were next. They wore sweaters, and Wagner had corduroy breeches.

"Cagno's Itala was pushed to the line. He looked nervous and seemed to be talking to his mechanic to overcome his self-consciousness. He went off well, the mechanic pumping up pressure furiously.

"Haynes (America), in a little 50-hp car, not different from the stock models in mechanical construction which are known as the Haynes, came up chewing gum. The mechanic cranked the engine, jumped into the car, and the machinery worked well. . . .

"Jenatzy was the first to round the course, with Lancia immediately after him. Tracy drew up in front of the stand and protested loudly against the crowd who were obstructing the road. As the result of a broken steering gear the F.I.A.T. of Weilschott left the road at a corner, and a boy who was struck by the car had several limbs broken.

"On the second round Wagner was at the head with Lancia and Jenatzy just behind, while Shepard, Duray, and Clement were struggling hard in the rear. At the end of the fifth lap, when at mid-course, Wagner was yet leading, with Lancia and Jenatzy still pressing hard. It was at this moment that unhappily several spectators were the victims of their indiscretion. At East Norwich Tracy's Locomobile skidded on a greasy corner and ran into a group of onlookers, upsetting a young man and crushing his legs. Shepard was blameless for a similar accident which forced him to abandon when holding fourth place. While his Hotchkiss was mounting the Manhasset Hill at a tremendous pace a spectator tried to cross the course right in

Lancia's F.I.A.T. at Manhasset Corner.

front of the car, which was on him like lightning. Shepard swung his car to one side, but could not avoid hitting him, hurling the body fifty feet away and causing instantaneous death.

"In spite of these and other melancholy incidents the strained enthusiasm did not seem to diminish as Wagner and Lancia continued to struggle for the lead. Wagner drove admirably and gradually increased his lead in the seventh and eighth rounds, and started on the last lap six minutes ahead of Lancia in time. Duray had now come up into third place. Intense excitement prevailed when Lancia flew past the winning post, but, as he had started fourth, Wagner had six minutes in which to arrive to beat the Italian.

"The seconds ticked slowly, and news spread that Wagner had had a breakdown, so that Darracq supporters began to feel nervous. Their fears were, however, soon dispelled as Wagner came in a burst of speed, crossing the line with three minutes in hand. . . . "

Thus came to a grisly end the last of the early Vanderbilt Cup races. Overexcitement among the spectators, lack of sufficient race control, deliberate sabotage among certain local people, and the outcry in the press against "the terrible slaughter of innocent people" forced Mr. Vanderbilt to end the series. The 1906 Vanderbilt Cup was the last of the great "dust-and-open-roads" events in America, as was the Paris-Madrid in Europe.

By Richard Hough, based
on the report in CAR
ILLUSTRATED *November, 1906*

VANDERBILT CUP 1906 RESULTS		
1ST	L. Wagner	Darracq 61.43 mph average
2ND	V. Lancia	F.I.A.T.
3RD	A. Duray	Lorraine-Dietrich

CHAPTER THREE:

The oldest event on the British motor racing calendar is the Royal Automobile Club's Tourist Trophy. It was first run in 1905. It had been started to demonstrate to the world the rugged quality of British automobiles, and to test them one against the other, and against foreign cars, in a long and hard race over a mountainous course on the Isle of Man, an island of granite rock and moorland and beautiful beaches situated midway between Ireland and Britain. British as well as several Continental and Ameri-

FASTEST AROUND THE — MOUNTAINS

can manufacturers recognized that victory in this highly publicized event would mean good business, and they spent much time and money preparing cars. But there was a strict limit to what they were allowed to do in the way of mechanical changes. For the Tourist Trophy was intended at first strictly as a stock car race, with only the smallest modifications to the cars, and gas consumption was considered almost as important as speed.

Most of the first T.T.s were won by sturdy and re-

liable touring cars that looked very little different from any of the high, open "horseless carriages" that you could buy in any showroom at that time. The bodywork was lighter, the engine was highly tuned, and the drivers themselves were a great deal bolder than those normally met on the roads. They wrapped themselves in great fur or waterproof coats, and wore goggles and caps back-to-front.

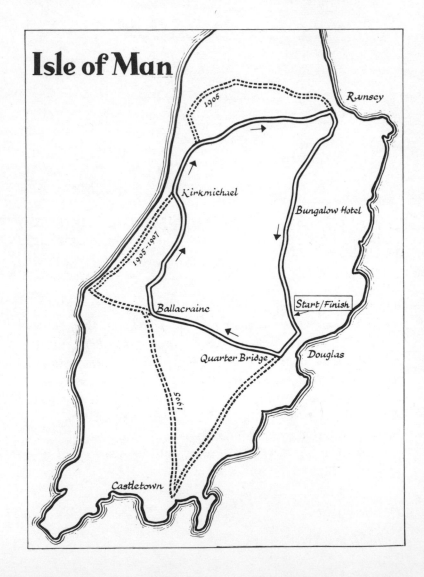

They were pioneer racing drivers, who considered an average speed around the mountainous 52-mile circuit of over 30 mph fast going! And so it was on those rough roads and with the crude, ineffective brakes of that time.

The first of these T.T.s was won by a two-cylinder Arrol-Johnston, a very curious car made in Scotland. It was driven by the car's designer, John S. Napier. The second event in 1906 was won by a make of car that has since become renowned throughout the world for qualities of refinement and superior engineering rather than speed: Rolls-Royce.

Soon the winning speed of the annual T.T. was rising toward 50 mph. The event was becoming world famous, and just as all the great motor-racing firms today always enter cars for the Tourist Trophy, so for the 1914 race there came team cars from Germany, Belgium, France, as well as Britain. It was one of the last motor races run in Europe before world war swept over the Continent. Some of the drivers, and the mechanics who helped to prepare and service the cars during the two-day race, were to be killed in the imminent war; others were to become famous in the world of motor manufacture and motor racing in the 1920s and 1930s. Two of the drivers were to be responsible in later years for the design of one of the greatest sports cars of all time. Their names were W. O. Bentley and F. T. Burgess, and the car they were later to work on together was of course the Bentley. Several more of the men who fought in the long 1914 T.T. were to drive in the Bentley team between 1922 and 1930, the years when they had their greatest successes.

The race, as you will see, was won by a car designed by the French designer Louis Coatalen, an engineer of *astonishing fluency and skill, who did his most celebrated work in Britain between 1910 and 1930. The cars that did best of all, as all three of the team survived, were the Belgian Minervas, a make very few people hear about today. Their engines were unusual in having sleeve valves. But the little D.F.P., a French car, should not be forgotten. For this was entered and driven by W. O. Bentley, and it went as fast and consistently as it did because of the special work he carried out on the engine and the chassis of this car. In its performance was to be seen the first evidence of the genius that was to flower fully some six years later.*

THE CHIEF CONTESTANTS	
DRIVERS	CARS
K. Lee Guinness *(Britain)*	Sunbeam 3.3 liters *(Britain)*
A. Guinness *(Britain)*	Sunbeam 3.3 liters *(Britain)*
G. Porporato *(Italy)*	Minerva 3.3 liters *(Belgium)*
L. Molon *(Italy)*	Minerva 3.3 liters *(Belgium)*
C. Riecken *(Belgium)*	Minerva 3.3 liters *(Belgium)*
F. T. Burgess *(Britain)*	Humber 3.3 liters *(Britain)*
R. S. Witchell *(Britain)*	Straker-Squire 3.2 liters *(Britain)*
W. O. Bentley *(Britain)*	D.F.P. 2.0 liters *(France)*

BY RICHARD HOUGH

It had been six years since the last Tourist Trophy, and in that time the motorcar had grown up and the racing car had reached an interesting stage of adolescence. The **T.T.** had developed from a race for standard-production cars to an event in which only light, out-and-out racing cars had any chance of success. Rarely again were the Straker-Squire, D.F.P., S.A.V.A., and others to appear on the European racing program; at the same time the double overhead-camshaft Vauxhalls designed by Laurence Pomeroy and Louis Coatalen's Sunbeams presaged a new age of high-revving, high-efficiency engines that were briefly glimpsed before the curtain of war fell over Europe.

Compared with a modern race on a short, special circuit like Watkins Glen, Sebring, or Indianapolis, this 1914 race might not be considered much of a spectacle. There were fewer than two dozen cars, which might be anywhere along the forty miles of road. As the race extended over two days and a high proportion of starters had retired by the end of the first day, there were long gaps on the second day where there were only the scoreboard and the blue-gray slopes of Snaefell Mountain to interest the spectators in the grandstand. But the people of the Isle of Man had never before seen anything to compare with this race, and no cars like these had ever before come to the island.

There were only two regulations for the race that mattered much. The engine capacity of the race cars was limited to 3,310 cc., the weight of any car to a minimum of 2,400 pounds. For the first time there were cash prizes in addition to the trophy itself. The *Daily Telegraph* had offered £1,000 to the winning driver, £250 to the driver who came second, and a £300 team prize. Another trophy, the Henry Edmunds Trophy, was to go to the fastest car over the 6 1/2-mile stretch from Ramsey to the Bungalow, a point high up on the slopes of Snaefell. Much of this climb had a 10 per cent gradient, though there was a fast slightly downhill section at the end.

The race of sixteen laps of the circuit was to be spread out over two days, June 10 and 11, making 600 miles in all. The roads were still almost entirely untarred and were quite inadequate for cars with top speeds over 90 mph. The narrow, humpbacked stone bridges at Ballig, Ballaugh, and Sulby, which had had to be treated carefully by much slower cars eight or nine years earlier, were now highly dangerous. At 30 mph the famous bump on Ballig Bridge sent the cars leaping several feet clear of its rough stone surface.

There were many interesting foreign entries among the cars, the Minervas and Adlers arousing particular curiosity. The former, from Belgium, were unique in having sleeve valves. The German Adlers made no pretense at being stock cars. They were out-and-out racers with very smooth and efficient-looking bodies ending with a huge egg-shaped tail like a bustle. Concealed in here were their spare wheels. They were painted white with red stripes and had "the best-finished upholstery that is to be found in any of the cars," as *The Autocar's* reporter described them. In the fashion of their day the piston stroke of their engines was enormously long, and like the Mercedes, they had a magneto driving gear across the end of the crankshaft, operating two magnetos. Details of their engines were hard to come by, and there was much curiosity about their gear ratios. One newspaperman concluded by the way they throbbed their way at well over 60 mph up Snaefell Mountain during practice that high gear must be very high. The Sunbeams, on the other hand, "screamed like demons," wrote *The Motor*.

There was never any mistaking the sleeve-valve Minervas during either practice or the race. Their oil smoke, caused by their auxiliary exhaust ports at the bottom of their cylinders, could be described only as prodigious. Some anxiety about this menace was expressed by other competitors, and W. O. Bentley remembers to this day the dark gray cloudy streaks of smoke that were almost impenetrable when driving into the low sun during dawn practice. The roads were narrow enough, the walls that bordered them hard enough, without having to cope with a smoke screen in order to get by other cars. Complaints were made to the Minerva team, and some mechanical adjustment reduced the density of the smoke slightly; but two days before the race they were still reported to be leaving "a blue film clean across the mountain from one horizon to the other."

No driver was encouraged by greater good will than W. O. Bentley from the time he landed at Douglas with his little polished aluminum D.F.P. Every other engine was at least half again as big, but none had had the meticulous preparation W. O. had given his Doriot, Flandrin et Parent. It was, as far as is known, the first car to be fitted with aluminum pistons, all the reciprocating parts had been lightened, and he had considerably raised the compression. To meet the regulations, W. O. had to use the axles of the larger model D.F.P., which added considerably to the

weight. "The monobloc engine," reported *The Autocar*, "is apparently unfaked and looks very innocent." "What does D.F.P. stand for? Why, Deserves First Place, of course" was what people in Douglas were saying. With ten laps of the racing circuit of Brooklands at 81.98 mph, and the flying half-mile at 89.7 mph to its credit only a few weeks before, victory did not seem outside the realm of possibility.

The Stars arrived painted a spectacular red. They had the standard sporting chassis and could do 96 mph with their engines running at 3,000 rpm.

In the Sunbeams Louis Coatalen's genius for adapting other peoples' ideas to his own use had flowered at its finest. With himself in charge of the team, the Guinness brothers and the wild Resta as drivers, they were considered almost unbeatable.

The only three Humber cars ever specially built for racing were led by their designer, F. T. Burgess. They were twin overhead camshaft machines, four valves per

One of the ill-fated Vauxhalls brakes
at Hillberry Corner.

cylinder, and produced about 100 brake horsepower at
3,200 rpm.

If any British car was going to beat the Sunbeams,
it would be a Vauxhall, many people thought. After being
seriously delayed, the Vauxhalls arrived, painted black and
looking very rakish and as light as in fact they were. By
eliminating the underframe, designer Laurence Pomeroy
had saved 63 pounds from the weight of the chassis. "The
extreme lightness," reported *The Autocar*, "has not been
achieved by the time-honored practice of boring a hole
wherever one could be bored, but by a combination of
broad treatment with almost microscopic attention to each
detail, which is much more difficult, though in the long run
much safer, more satisfactory, and far more likely to tend
toward permanent improvement in design." The engines
had twin overhead camshafts, each shaft on ball bearings,
with forced-feed lubrication. The cylinders were monobloc
cast; the crankshafts were carefully balanced, but as a result of overhasty preparation one threw a balance weight

53

in practice on the last day, wrecking two connecting rods and piercing a hole in the top crankcase chamber. By dint of all-night work by candlelight the car was on the line the next morning—and a rousing reception it received from the crowd. It was a hectic few days for Pomeroy, for A. J. Hancock's car was found to be 50 pounds underweight on the weigh bridge. For this, however, the cure was simpler. Pomeroy dashed off down the road and returned with a road worker and a sack of stones!

Practice was from first light to 7 A.M. These were the only hours during which the drivers were allowed on the course, even on foot. It rained as it so often does in the Isle of Man. This year it rained continuously, and up on the mountains the wind was at gale force. The spectators did not seem to care, however; they collected in little frozen groups at most of the corners and had a fair measure of entertainment, especially at Ballaugh Bridge where the light Vauxhalls took spectacular leaps. Kenelm Lee Guinness bent his Sunbeam's frame and front axle in a crash by the Bungalow. But this was less serious than Wilhelm's collision with a wall at 55 mph, which put him and his mechanic into the hospital, and brought the reserve Adler onto the starting line. A rare shaft of blinding dawn sunshine appearing suddenly over the horizon ahead of him caused Bianchi to spin through two complete circles as he crossed Sulby Bridge in his car.

It was still pelting with rain and blowing half a gale on race morning, and though it had stopped by breakfast, the dust-laying calcium chloride which some misguided official had ordered to be put down prevented the surface from drying out. This chemical also caused some drivers and mechanics severe pain when it splashed up into their eyes during the race. Mud was obviously going to be a real problem, and some of the mechanics were soon busy wiring on makeshift plyboard mudguards to provide some degree of protection for the drivers.

From the start-finish area at Bray Hill the road ran downhill toward Quarter Bridge a mile away. And down here at 11 o'clock in the morning, with the sun at last beginning to break through, the champion driver Porporato accelerated away, trailing a cloud of characteristic oil smoke from the exhaust of his Minerva. Burgess's own pretty Humber was next off, sounding brutishly healthy. Kenelm Lee Guinness took the first of the Sunbeams away two minutes later. The first Star, Hancock's Vauxhall, and Adler number one followed, and then W. O. Bentley in his little D.F.P.

The current holder of the Tourist Trophy, W. Watson, got only as far as Union Mills a few miles from the start when the crankshaft of his Vauxhall broke. Nor did the Sunbeam team manage a single lap intact, Resta going out with a rattling big end bolt at Ramsey. But for the gay young Guinness brothers, in the other two Sunbeams, everything went right. Kenelm got around the circuit—along the winding narrow roads, up into the mountains, and down again—at a record speed of 58.9 mph, and his brother Algy overtook six cars and managed two minutes faster time than anyone else. Porporato was third best, then the Straker-Squires showed they were faster than most people had expected.

It was very soon evident that the winner was going to be found among the Belgian Minervas, or the British Sunbeams and Straker-Squires, whose overhead camshaft engines, designed by Roy Fedden, were giving over 80 hp at

3,200 rpm. By the end of the third lap the first and second Adlers were both out of the running, and so was Tuck's Humber.

For the next four hours there was little change in the position. The Minervas could make no more impression on the Sunbeams, and only Witchell (who was later to become works manager at Bentley Motors) threatened the Belgian cars in any way. Lisle overdid it at Ballaugh Bridge and badly damaged his Star. Once Kenelm came down Bray Hill a shade over the safe limit in his Sunbeam, but sensibly recognized this fact as he went into the right-angled corner just before the grandstand. Luckily there was an escape road ready for him, and he rushed down this for half a mile, to cheers from the spectators, before turning and rejoining the race.

Otherwise the two Guinness brothers, lapping with admirable regularity in the blazing sun, looked unassailable, and they had a clear lead at the end of the first day's racing, when these were the positions of the first five cars:

K. Lee Guinness	Sunbeam	5 hr. 15 min.
A. Guinness	Sunbeam	5 " 18 "
G. Porporato	Minerva	5 " 31 "
C. Riecken	Minerva	5 " 32 "
R. Witchell	Straker-Squire	5 " 33 "

The first day's racing had been disastrous for the Vauxhalls. After such hasty preparation and only one day's practice, trouble could have been expected. But now they had only one car left in the race, and its carburetor was popping and a broken water pipe had already delayed it for twenty minutes.

One of the Straker-Squires
at the beginning climb up to the mountain.

W. J. BRUNELL PHOTO

To everyone's surprise the sun shone again the next morning. The cars had been locked up and under guard all night, and they eventually emerged for the start in exactly the condition they were in when the previous day's racing had ceased, filthy dirty, unserviced, with fuel tanks almost empty and tires worn smooth. From the starting line they were released at three-minute intervals in the order in which they had finished the evening before. First away was Kenelm Lee Guinness, and he and his mechanic immediately became involved in the strenuous business of pushing their Sunbeam from the starting line back to the Sunbeam pit. The mechanic took off the filler cap and loosened the straps holding the spare tires to the car, while Kenelm poured in

57

the gas through an outsize funnel and checked the oil and water levels. Then they both worked together on the tires and in six minutes were ready. Kenelm hopped into the driving seat and pushed the offside rear wheel with one hand while the mechanic heaved from behind. At 10 mph the engine fired, the mechanic leapt in—and the leaders were away.

Kenelm's brother, Algy, was already at his pit with the second Sunbeam, and Porporato was just settling down to the exhausting task of pouring ten gallons of oil into the sump of his Minerva. "So that's where all the smoke's coming from!" murmured voices in the crowd as can after can was emptied into the engine.

Five minutes later the pollution of the Manx air began once again. Trailing a great cloud of oil smoke, Porporato charged off down Bray Hill. The Minervas were always most spectacular before their engines warmed up; but once they had achieved a working temperature, they were the only cars in the race that neither spat on the overrun nor misfired on the initial burst of throttle when accelerating away from the corners.

Hancock spent nearly an hour on his carburetor before his slim black Vauxhall got away. Witchell, fast at his pit and even faster on his first lap, succeeded in knocking off the 40-second advantage with which Porporato had started and actually got ahead of him on time. Behind the two Sunbeams the first real drama of the race was played out over the next two hours. The solitary Straker-Squire was fighting hard against the entire Minerva team, sometimes getting ahead of them all and then falling back again as the Belgians struggled harder than ever. Then at the very beginning of the fourth lap of the day misfortune

The sun is out at last as K. Lee Guinness
races his winning Sunbeam toward the finish line.

W. J. BRUNELL PHOTO

struck Witchell hard. He had only just got past the pits on Bray Hill when his engine died. A glance under the hood told him the gas pipe had broken, and he was probably the only driver in the race without a spare on board. He sent his mechanic running back a quarter mile to the pits. But there was not one there either. There was a moment of total dismay when this discovery was made. Then Louis Coatalen, the Sunbeam chief, appeared from the adjoining pit like a good Samaritan with a spare pipe and some wire from his own supplies and presented them to Witchell's mechanic, who went running off with them to his

59

car. Driver and mechanic worked frenziedly under the hood and were away again in the race, having lost only fifteen minutes.

The appearance of the Sunbeams past the grandstands every forty minutes had been so regular that it was with something of a shock that the crowd realized that Algy in the second team car had lost station five minutes behind his brother. The Sunbeam was followed by the three Minervas—but no second Sunbeam. At last the news trickled in. It seemed that Algy had had to stop several times before reaching Ramsey, and then had had to retire with the most trivial complaint to his car. The lubricating pipe to his rear universal had broken, and the joint had seized solid. Now it rested with his brother alone to hold off the strong Belgian opposition that was pressing so hard.

At the end of the thirteenth lap on the second day's racing these were the positions:

K. Lee Guinness	*Sunbeam*	8 hr.	36 min.		40 sec.	
C. Riecken	*Minerva*	8 "	55 "		59 "	
G. Porporato	*Minerva*	8 "	59 "		42 "	
L. Molon	*Minerva*	9 "	19 "		50 "	
R. Witchell	*Straker-Squire*	9 "	20 "		35 "	
W. Wright	*Humber*	9 "	47 "		5 "	
W. Bentley	*D.F.P.*	10 "	6 "		8 "	

But Witchell continued to drive brilliantly and was creeping up on all the Minervas as he made up his lost time. He got past Molon and Porporato, and at the beginning of the last lap of this marathon race was in third place. He was gaining fast on the leading Minerva as he rushed through Ramsey town and began the long climb up into the mountains. Ahead of him Hancock had at last got his Vauxhall going again and was in the process of proving at least that the car was fast, if unreliable. Alas! Constant worries and troubles over two successive days proved too much for him. It was his judgment that was to let him down this time. He went into a left-hander too fast and skidded. The car thrust its way through a dry-stone wall and took to the heather, tearing up the ground as it slid along on its side at some 60 mph before coming to a halt.

The doctor's car was summoned from down the road, and it set off with the stretcher party just as Witchell's Straker-Squire hove into sight, going great guns. Witchell was flagged down, and for six agonizing minutes crawled up the narrow road behind the doctor's car. After he had at last got by, there was no chance of making up the time, and Molon took third place ahead of him with a margin of just thirty seconds, which is fine enough over a total distance of more than 600 miles.

All the other cars in the race except the three Minervas, the winning Sunbeam, and Witchell's Straker-Squire either had crashed or had retired through mechanical trouble. But there was one exception. Forty-five minutes behind the last Minerva came the little silver D.F.P. W.O. Bentley had had not a moment's anxiety as he went round and round the long course at just under 50 mph. "As far as we were concerned, it was almost boring," he commented.

And so ended, on a gray summer's afternoon in 1914, the fastest of the great classic Tourist Trophy races run on the Around-the-Mountains Isle of Man course. Six weeks later war came to Europe. All motor racing ceased, and for many of those who had taken part it was the last motor race of all.

An incident recounted to a newspaper reporter after the race by the winning driver, Kenelm Lee Guinness:

For some reason even unknown to himself, friend Cook (my mechanic) took it into his head to get out of his seat to have a look at the back tire on my side, choosing the approach to Ballaugh Bridge for his inspection. We were on the bridge before I had a chance to do anything. He shot clean up in the air, and I thought it was all up with him. However, I had momentarily forgotten Newton's laws of motion. He landed back with his nose first—on my head—luckily only a glancing blow. Poor Cook got a nasty bump. However, he managed to get himself back into the car again and soon made light of his harrowing experience. He said it was a good omen as we had drawn first blood.

TOURIST TROPHY, *1957*

TOURIST TROPHY 1914 RESULTS		
1st	K. Lee Guinness	Sunbeam 56.44 mph average
2nd	C. Riecken	Minerva
3rd	L. Molon	Minerva

CHAPTER FOUR:

Harry Miller and Fred Duesenberg—those two men were the greatest automobile engineers in America in the 1920s. Their machines were to provide the closest competitive racing all over the U.S.A. for many years, and nowhere more excitingly than at the thirteenth annual "500" at Indianapolis's "brickyard."

Miller had built his first successful engine in 1922. Like the Duesenberg, it was a straight-eight; Miller refined

FASTEST AROUND THE - BRICKYARD

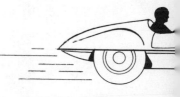

his and obtained more power by using a valve gear incorporating two overhead camshafts. He put his engine in a Duesenberg chassis, and the brilliant Duesenberg driver Jimmy Murphy drove it to its first major victory at Indianapolis at a record speed of 94.48 mph. Two years later Murphy persuaded Miller to build him a new car with drive to the front, instead of the rear, wheels. The canny Murphy calculated that this form of transmission would

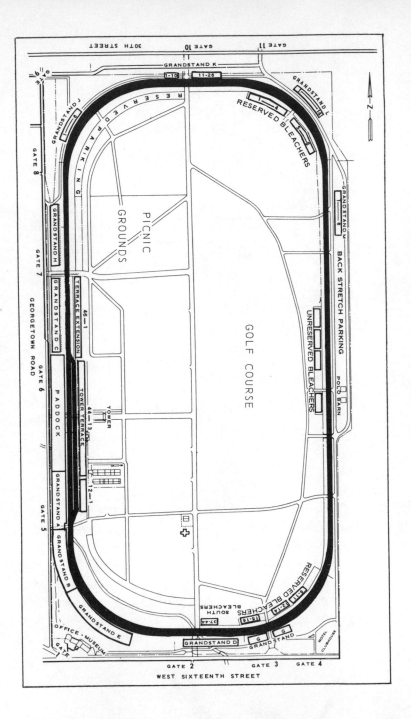

provide better road-holding and give him a great advan-
tage on the Indianapolis curves. He never lived to discover
the proof of his theory, for he was killed in a race at Syra-
cuse, New York, later that year.

Murphy's car was entered by Miller for the 1925
Indianapolis. More orthodox Millers were also running,
and these were preferred to the little front-drive car by
drivers like Harry Hartz, Leon Duray, and Bennett Hill.
The only pilot Miller could persuade to drive the new ma-
chine, the Junior Eight Special as it was called, was the
steady veteran Dave Lewis. But as you can read from this
on-the-spot account, the ingenious low-slung front-driver
was the sensation of the race. As it showed its pace and
steady cornering in the hands of Dave Lewis, it was Ben-
nett Hill who suddenly changed his mind and took over the
wheel when the elderly Lewis, exhausted from his sensa-
tional run for more than 400 miles, had to give up the cock-
pit.

Pete De Paolo in his Duesenberg managed to scrape
home the winner. But Dave Lewis's magnificent drive in the
new car was a momentous occasion both for Harry Miller
and for Fred Duesenberg, whose machines were soon to
lose the grip they had gained on American track racing.
Nor was that all. Besides forcing De Paolo to such a speed
that for the first time ever Indianapolis was won at over
the hundred mark (a record unbroken during the 1920s),
the front-driven Junior Eight with its brilliant transmis-
sion and suspension systems set off a train of technical in-
novations that were to play a big part in the mechanical
improvement and greater safety of passenger automobiles
for many years to come.

THE CHIEF CONTESTANTS	
DRIVERS	CARS
Pete De Paolo	Duesenberg
Dave Lewis	Junior Eight Special (Front-Drive Miller)
Harry Hartz	Miller
P. Shafer	Duesenberg
Earl Cooper	Miller
Leon Duray	Miller
(all cars and drivers American)	

BY CLARENCE PHILLIPS

Indianapolis is all set for the thirteenth annual grind on the celebrated brick speedway. As usual, only more so, the city is packed with people from all points of the compass. The weather bureau promises good racing weather but likely it will be hot out here at the track. Last year when we saw Joe Boyer and L. L. Corum wheel a Duesenberg to victory it was chilly enough for light overcoats.

Right now, at eight o'clock, you can hear any sort of speculations. Many questions are being put which only the end of the race will answer.

For one thing, people are wondering what the front-wheel drive will do. It will be driven by Dave Lewis—the Junior Eight Special. While Lewis did not make anything like the time Duray, De Paolo, and Hartz did in the trials, there's an idea in some quarters that the front-wheel drive will step up with or ahead of the flock in actual battle.

Then, here and there you find strong Fiat boosters. They think Bordino has more than a fair chance. Also what about Duray?

Duray certainly showed a lead foot in the trials, grabbing the pole position at an average of 113.19 miles an hour. Right behind him by an eyelash in the trials, Pete De Paolo, the Duesy flyer, made a strong bid for notice. Pete's record makes him look good, and it might be said that he is easily one of the high favorites. As for the records, though, there are others in the race. Tommy Milton at last count stood at the head of this year's class on points. Up in the high group also were Cooper, Hartz, and Bennie Hill.

The way the betting odds stand now you can't do better than even money on any of the favorites. "That Fiat is really dangerous," an eminent technical man just hissed in my ear. Another for the Fiat.

Bordino's red Fiat, No. 22, is the first race car out on the bricks. It is headed for the pit. Only 8:55 now. The fuss begins at 10, and sharp, according to the tradition. Crowds are pouring in in spite of the fact that the place looks jammed already.

Airplanes are sailing overhead and movie men are grinding their picture mills. Many thousands have lunch boxes with them—here for the day.

A rabbit scared up from somewhere is running down

the track. He keeps on running on the bricks because there is no place for the poor devil to turn out and the whoops of the stands only make him set back his ears and beat it all the harder. "It's the pacemaker," wheezes my technical friend.

He's wrong this time, though, for the pacemaker, Eddie Rickenbacker, in a car bearing his own name, comes in front of the press stand.

The announcer tells us that M. C. Jones will drive No. 7, the Skelly Special, with Fred Harder as relief driver. We'd like to have this thing start.

More information from the megaphone. The Super Ford Special, with Belt aboard, was scratched, as was the Smith Special, which was to be piloted by Harry Thickstein, and Tom Alley's Kess Line Special.

That leaves 22 starters. Last year 21; still it is a small field. It is small but it is high class. Crowd estimated now at 145,000, including the several gentlemen pushing me from behind.

There goes the first bomb. The race will be on in 20 minutes. The drivers are forming in position. Duray, in his Miller job, takes the pole.

Another bomb. Drivers and mechanics gather in center of the track to be photographed. Howard C. Marmon, of the board of judges, forecasts an average of 102 miles per hour. Also that the winning car will have only one tire change—in the right rear.

The mechanics are cranking up. There is the roar of engines raring to go and plenty of smoke. Not as much smoke, though, as in the old days.

Seth Klein, starter, comes out on his roost with the red flag.

The pacemaker starts—the pack is on his heels and the game is under way.

To add to the thrill of the start two airplanes are zooming over the stands.

Necks are stretched southward and the crowds yell as the drivers flash over the bricks past the stands. Peter De Paolo, in a Duesenberg, is in the lead; Duray, in a Miller, is next and then Harry Hartz, in a Miller.

The leaders are close together and, of course, the entire crowd well bunched. No one was left at the post on the start. Pete De Paolo did have a hard time getting off and surprised the crowd when he leaped into the lead on one round after that handicap. The Jones-Whitaker, with Herbert Jones at the wheel, is tagging the crowd.

Frank Elliott, in a Miller, goes to the pit. First pit stop. The Skelly Special, handled by M. C. Jones next to the pit. First lap was made in 1:26:65 at the rate of 104 mph. Last year Joe Boyer reeled it off at 98.39 mph but got into trouble as a consequence. The first two laps were made at an average of 104.80 mph.

On the fourth lap De Paolo is well in the lead. Duray still second; Earl Cooper, in a Miller, third; Hartz, in a Miller, fourth; and Ralph Hepburn, in a Miller, fifth. The race is just getting well under way. Cooper is stepping out like he means business.

Cooper has passed Duray and taken second place. Earl is still going fast. The first 10 miles was clipped off in 5:45:04.

Bordino with the Fiat goes to the pits. His supercharger is the noisiest one on the place.

De Paolo has a 200-yard lead and Cooper is hotly followed by Duray. Fred Comer, in a Miller, is moving up.

Bordino is away from the pits again—stopped for 55 seconds, changed spark plugs. Cooper is increasing his lead on Duray. Frank Elliott to the pits for spark plugs. De Paolo increases his lead over Cooper—Duray is about 100 yards behind Earl.

Announcer says the Jones-Whitaker stopped on a flag for instructions. The first 25 miles was reeled off in 14:24:09—De Paolo leading. Skelly Special drops in on pitmen again, this time to change spark plugs.

Positions of leaders at end of first 25 miles: De Paolo, Cooper, Hartz, Duray, Lewis, Hepburn, Ellingboe, Shafer, Milton, Mourre. Last year an average of 99.15 mph was made for this distance. They are galloping along five miles faster than last year.

De Paolo's car is smoking some. Ralph De Palma, in his Miller, slows down at pit, points to a tire, and goes on by. Next time around finds Ralph at pits. De Paolo laps Shattuck in a Miller. Pete now on his 18th lap. De Palma spent 50 seconds at pit for shock absorber adjustment. Moss is now driving Jones-Whitaker Special for Herbert Jones's relief. The first fifty was run at an average rate of 104.13 mph. De Paolo laps Mourre. He is about 14 seconds ahead of Cooper. Pete is running like a watch. Hill to the pits.

Bordino, the Italian driver and only foreign entrant, is two laps behind De Paolo. Pete dashes by several of his competitors, the crowd cheers, and Cooper seems to be gaining right now on De Paolo.

Bennie Hill goes to pits for shock absorber adjustment and is out in one minute and twenty-five seconds. Ellingboe goes into pits for same purpose and is off in one minute and ten seconds.

Ellingboe sheered a key on the steering gear and his car, a Miller Special, is out of the race. First car to get out. The clash at this point is between De Paolo and Cooper. Harder has taken the helm of the Skelly, its second relief.

De Paolo lapped his Uncle Ralph at 75 miles. The positions at 75 miles of the first group: De Paolo, Cooper, Hartz, Lewis, Duray, Shafer, Hepburn, Mourre, De Vore, Milton.

The pencil-thin Duesenberg, winner in 1925,
and the first car to average over the 100-mph mark.
Driver Pete De Paolo in the cockpit.
INDIANAPOLIS MOTOR SPEEDWAY PHOTO

Skelly again to pit. Cooper is closing the distance between himself and the leader. The fight is still between Pete and Earl. Neither has gained much additional advantage in some time, although they are seesawing considerably. Lewis, in the front-wheel drive, is making a steady race, now in fourth position and gaining on Hartz in third.

Ellingboe has relieved Hill in a Miller. The car is not in the first ten of the field at this time.

M. C. Jones again takes wheel of the Skelly.

The first 100 miles was zipped off in 57:44:94 at an average of 103.89 mph. Last year's average: 98.35 mph. They are traveling. Positions: De Paolo, Cooper, Hartz, Shafer, Lewis, Duray, Hepburn, De Vore, Mourre, Milton.

De Paolo, Cooper, and Hartz have been holding well to their present positions. Shafer has come from sixth place to fourth in his Duesy. McDonogh was sent to pits by broken truss rod and for gas. Shafer passes Cooper for second place. A race is on between Shafer and Pete, his stable mate. They are doing some interesting grinding.

Time for 125 miles: 1:12:12.18. Average: 103.87 mph. Last year's average: 98.43 mph.

Shafer passes De Paolo and takes first position. The fans yell. Everyone watches to see how the chase will stand on the next turn. They pass us, Shafer 75 yards ahead. The Duesenberg stable sits pretty at this period. Cooper, in third place, is a quarter of a mile behind. Bordino now three laps behind. Mourre goes to pits.

Time for 150 miles is 1:26:22 at an average of 104.20 mph. Last year's average: 98.36 mph. Skelly to the pits again. Duray is slipping. Held fifth place for some time, but now in sixth.

Ellingboe, driving Bennie Hill's mount, turned

around three times at north turn when right rear tire went flat. On 61st lap Ira Vail visits pits.

De Paolo has jumped back into the lead amid howls from the stands. The boy is popular. Ellingboe puts in one minute and twenty-eight seconds at pits for tire, gas, oil, and adjustments.

Bennie Hill driving No. 3 again. Vail passes out of the picture with the R. J. Special with broken rod. Skelly goes to pit.

Time at 175 miles: 1:40:47.26. Average: 104.18 mph. Last year 98.36 mph was the average. Order: De Paolo, Shafer, Hartz, Lewis, Cooper, Duray, Hepburn, Milton, Bordino, Mourre.

Carlens relieves Hill. Hartz goes from fourth to third place. Cooper slumps from third to fourth. These changes in the last 25 miles.

Bordino goes to pit. Jones relieves Moss in Jones-Whitaker job. Shafer's right rear tire flat. Cooper passes Shafer during former's pit stop. Shafer off again but lost lap to De Paolo, who is leading. Right rear tire goes flooey for Pete Kreis in a Duesy. The right rears are catching it. That was predicted. The turns on these bricks are especially hard on them.

Mourre, who was relieved by Gleason, is driving for Bordino in the Fiat. Bordino injured hand and went to hospital.

Some excitement on the south stretch. It develops that the Jones-Whitaker car, driven by Herb Jones, hit the wall and caught fire, Jones jumping out and escaping injury. The car is out of it.

There are 18 drivers in the race now out of 22 starters.

Time at 200 miles: 1:25:36.89. Average: 103.79 mph.

Last year's average: 98.38 mph. Looks like a track record again is on the way. Order at this time: De Paolo, Hartz, Lewis, Duray, Hepburn, Shafer, Cooper, Milton, Kreis, Gleason (driving for Mourre).

Hartz passes De Paolo on the 86th lap. In the last 25 miles Lewis has come up to third from fifth place. The front-wheel drive is working well.

Now De Paolo passes Hartz and again takes first place. Elliott to pits. Tire trouble. De Paolo lengthens lead over Lewis. De Palma is six laps behind his flashing nephew, De Paolo.

Haibe takes Elliott's seat on No. 27, a Miller.

Time at 225 miles: 2:10:12.2. Average: 103.68 mph. Last year's average: 98.63 mph. Positions: De Paolo, Hartz, Cooper, Lewis, Hepburn, Duray, Shafer, Milton, Gleason, Kreis.

Hartz goes to pits. Right rear tire. Shafer to pits. Ditto. Jerry Wonderlich now driving for Bennie Hill. Jones-Whitaker is back in race after the fire. Referee rules it can continue.

Time at 250 miles: 2:24:59.31. Average: 103.45 mph. Last year's average: 98.78 mph. Order: De Paolo, Lewis, Hepburn, Duray, Shafer, Hartz, Milton, Gleason, Shattuck.

De Paolo goes to pit for new right rear tire. Hartz hits wall at south turn, with blown right rear tire. Not hurt. Right rears continue to go. These are all balloon tires today. Their introduction at the Indianapolis track.

Lewis is now in the lead as De Paolo stops at pit. The Jones-Whitaker is out of the race.

Norman Batten is now driving for De Paolo, the latter having blistered his hands.

Hepburn is in lead at 108th lap. Wade Morton, now driving Mourre's original mount, goes to pits.

Time at 275 miles: 2:41:36.48. Average: 102.10 mph. Last year's average: 98.08 mph. Order: Hepburn, Cooper, Shafer, Batten, Lewis, Hartz, Milton, Morton, Kreis, De Palma.

Comer relieves Duray. Eighteen cars still in race. The scene has shifted considerably in the front ranks. Gleason now driving the Mourre mount. Morton getting out. Schultz is driving for Earl De Vore in a Miller. De Palma goes to pits, followed by Hepburn on his 116th round. Milton to pits.

L. L. Corum, co-winner with Boyer last year, relieves De Palma in a Miller. Hepburn holds lead.

Ellingboe, in a Miller Special originally driven by Bennie Hill, is out of race on 68th lap. Broke rear spring and had bearing trouble. Duray took on oil, gas, and two tires in thirty seconds.

Time at 300 miles: 2:56:88.50. Average: 101.95 mph. Last year's average: 98.17 mph. Order: Hepburn, Cooper, Shafer, Batten (for De Paolo), Lewis, Hartz, Milton, Kreis, Gleason, Duray.

Hepburn loses lead to Cooper on 121st lap when former stops at pits for gas, oil, and water—also right front and right rear tires. Off again in 35 seconds.

Cooper is leading nicely. Has not been to pit yet.

Cooper just hit the wall on south turn—his 124th lap. Wasn't hurt.

Lewis goes into lead, with Cooper out, followed by Batten in De Paolo's chariot and Hepburn.

De Paolo is back in No. 12, replacing Batten, who relieved him. He is in third place.

Time at 325 miles: 3:12:51.97. Average: 101.11 mph. Average last year: 97.77 mph. Order: Lewis, Shafer, Hepburn, DePaolo, Hartz, Milton, Kreis, Gleason, Duray, Corum (for De Palma).

De Paolo has come up to third place, but Lewis has a long lead. De Paolo is moving ahead like a bullet. Kreis goes to pit.

Elliott, who was relieved by Haibe, is again driving the No. 27 Miller.

Time at 350 miles: 3:27:23.24. Average: 101.26 mph. Last year's average: 98.01 mph. Order: Lewis, Shafer, De Paolo, Hepburn, Hartz, Milton, Kreis, Gleason, Duray, Corum (for De Palma).

Bennie Hill is driving McDonogh's Miller. De Paolo passes Shafer and chases Lewis. Comer is in No. 5, his own mount. Hepburn gets third position temporarily, but Shafer takes it from him. Hartz to fourth position. Tommy Milton crawls up a notch to fifth place. Lewis, the leader, is on his 149th lap.

De Paolo continues to gain on the front-wheel drive. Shafer is a lap and a half behind Lewis, in third place.

Time at 375 miles: 3:42:01.15. Average: 101.34 mph. Last year's average: 98.34 mph. Order: Lewis, De Paolo, Shafer, Hartz, Milton, Gleason, Duray, Kreis, Corum (for De Palma), Mourre (for Bordino).

Lewis has held lead since the 325-mile mark was reached.

De Palma now driving No. 8 again. Corum stepping out.

McDonogh now driving No. 14 again, replacing Bennie Hill, who relieved him.

Shafer goes to pits on 160th lap. Trouble of some

sort at north end of track. People standing up and looking.

Time at 400 miles: 3:56:30.20. Average: 101.48 mph. Last year's average: 98.21 mph. Lewis, De Paolo, and Shafer still lead.

Morton driving No. 9 for Phil Shafer—a Duesenberg.

Bordino is again driving the Fiat.

Here's the report of the accident that's been bothering us. No. 23, a Duesenberg Special driven by Gleason as relief, hit a side wall. Car is out of the race, but Gleason is uninjured.

Elliott was in the pits eleven seconds for a tire change.

Time at 425 miles: 4:11:14.52. Average: 101.49 mph. Last year's average: 98.36 mph. Lewis, De Paolo, Shafer, Hartz, Milton, and Duray are heading the procession.

Lewis slows down as if to stop at pit, but does not stop. Goes on around. Lewis stops at pit on 173rd lap and De Paolo again takes the lead.

Hill drives the front-wheel job for Lewis.

Shafer goes to second place. Hill is third and Hartz and Milton next in order. Hill takes in after the two ahead of him, but he is little more than a lap behind Pete. It is warming up into a race. Hill is stepping on the gas with a heavy foot.

On the 181st lap Pete finds Bennie still fighting to overhaul him but Pete now widens distance. Bennie is some 150 yards behind Pete—plus a lap. The crowd is excited. It wants to see a good finish and the end is not far off now.

Time at 450 miles: 4:26:28.87. Average: 101.32 mph. Last year's average: 98.18 mph. Order: De Paolo, Hill (for Lewis), Morton (for Shafer), Hartz, Milton, Duray, Kreis, Shattuck, De Palma, Bordino.

*Little Pete De Paolo, gallant victor
of the 1925 Indianapolis 500.*
INDIANAPOLIS MOTOR SPEEDWAY PHOTO

Fifty more miles to go. The question is, Will the
front-wheel drive be able to overtake De Paolo in so short
a distance? Pete has a lap to the good and is breezing along
at a rapid clip.

But look at that Junior Eight! It certainly takes the
turns beautifully. On the 184th lap the Junior Eight takes
in considerable slack. It looks like an almost impossible

thing for Hill to do the trick. A little pit trouble for Pete, however, and it might be all off for him as to first place.

Hill nearly overtakes Pete in front of the stands. The fans are yelling again. They like this sort of stuff. Hill is about to go by Pete at the turn when the little Duesy driver ties a brick on his foot and shoots around the curve ahead, and a lap to the good on Bennie.

A thrilling finish is in sight even if Peter has this lap to the good. On the 188th lap De Paolo and Hill continue to fight. Morton, driving for Shafer in third place, is about two laps behind.

The people in the stands are on their feet, yelling. Bennie and Peter are about abreast. Around they come again. Now the Junior Eight is about 100 yards ahead of Pete and going at a terrific rate. Pete still has nearly a lap to the good on the 500-mile distance.

Again they swing around in front of us. Not much change in relative positions, but both are moving mighty fast. Hill is gaining rapidly.

On the 196th lap De Paolo is only a half a lap ahead of Hill. Hill goes by. It seems like Pete is a long while coming along. The suspense makes everything quiet, save for the zooming of the different cars as they rush past. You can't keep from wondering if De Paolo has had trouble.

But by us he comes, his car apparently in good order. The answer to his late arrival is found likely in two places. First, in the high speed of the Junior Eight, and next in a possible signal from his pit to take it easy and not burn up his mount now. For, barring accident, he seems to have the race tucked away.

De Paolo starts on the 199th lap. Seth Klein, the starter, is ready with flags. De Paolo is given the green flag. More yelling. The last lap of De Paolo's distance is started.

The checkered flag is waved as De Paolo dashes past the finish line. How they yell! Peter continues the grind as a safeguard against misunderstanding—then is given a big ovation as he drifts up toward Fred Duesenberg and the Duesenberg pits.

He made a new record for the Indianapolis speedway, stepping off the distance in 4 hours 56 minutes and 39.47 seconds. His average speed was 101.13 mph against 98.23 made last year by the Boyer-Corum team, also in a Duesenberg, the best previous record.

Hill, driving the front-wheel-drive Junior Eight for Dave Lewis, finished in 4:57:33.15 at an average of 100.82 mph. Morton, driving a Duesenberg for Shafer, finished in 4:59:26.79 at an everage of 100.18 mph. Hartz finished with an average of 98.89 mph in fourth place, and the first four beat the record made last year. It was a fine exhibition of speed and crafty driving. The next problem is to get out of this mob and back to the hotel.

MOTOR AGE, *June 4, 1925*

INDIANAPOLIS 500 MILE 1925 RESULTS		
1ST	Pete De Paolo N. Batten	Duesenberg 101.13 mph average
2ND	Dave Lewis B. Hill	Junior Eight Special
3RD	W. Morton P. Shafer	Duesenberg

CHAPTER FIVE:

European Grand Prix racing between two world wars can be conveniently divided into two phases. The first phase ran from 1919 until the early months of 1934, and the second was heralded by the arrival of an entirely new and revolutionary form of Grand Prix car from Germany, described in the next chapter. The first phase was governed by several different sets of rules and regulations, called formula, *concerning the engine size, weight of car, etc., and saw the almost total supremacy of the French Bugatti*

FASTEST IN AFRICA –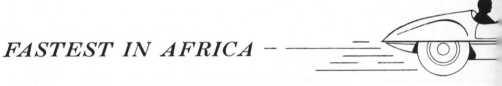

at one stage, the arrival of the Alfa Romeo and Maserati to dispute the laurels, the dominance of the 1½ liter Delage for a short period, and fleeting successes by the American Duesenberg and British Sunbeam.

By May, 1934, the era was nearly at an end, and a glorious new one was to open. But before the Italian and French cars yielded—after a tremendous struggle—to the new German cars, the fastest road race anywhere up to that time was held on a beautiful circuit, outside Tripoli

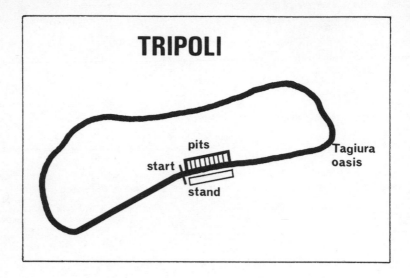

TRIPOLI

in North Africa. It is here described by Barré Lyndon, the best contemporary writer on motor racing.

Enzo Ferrari, whose cars we know so well today, was at this time running his own team of Alfa Romeos called Scuderia Ferrari. He had some of the best Italian drivers under his control, as well as Guy Moll and Louis Chiron from France. The blue-team Bugatti machines were driven by two more of France's top drivers. Whitney Straight was—and is today—a wealthy American sportsman who was one of the top drivers of the time. And, as you will read, two American Indianapolis cars and their drivers made history by entering for this race.

In Chapter 10 there are a few comments on the differences between European and American racing, and in the race described there the American Indianapolis cars utterly defeated the European road racing cars on a specially constructed track. *In the account that follows can be seen what happened when American cars, never designed for road racing but specifically for circulating at high speed around the brickyard, challenged the top road racing cars of Europe* on a road circuit. *That they did so well in a role for which they were never intended casts great credit on the determination of their drivers.*

THE CHIEF CONTESTANTS	
DRIVERS	CARS
A. Varzi (Italy)	Alfa Romeo 2.6 liters
G. Moll (France)	Alfa Romeo 2.6 liters
L. Chiron (France)	Alfa Romeo 2.6 liters
H. C. Hamilton (Britain)	Maserati 2.9 liters
W. Straight (U.S.A.)	Maserati 2.9 liters
G. E. T. Eyston (Britain)	Alfa Romeo 2.6 liters
P. Taruffi (Italy)	Maserati 4 liters
(all cars Italian)	

BY BARRÉ LYNDON

The North African event was held on Sunday, May 6, on the circuit which lies between Tripoli itself and the small town of Tagiura. In shape the course is oblong and encloses the Mellaha salt lake, which lends its name to the circuit, although the official title is *Circuito Permanente di Tripoli*. Part of the course is formed by the road between Tripoli and Tagiura, offering a stretch some three miles long which, however, is not absolutely straight. It starts from a corner by the Tagiura oasis and runs slightly downhill to the grandstands, set about a mile and a half from the corner; on the way the road runs through two sweeping curves. It then continues for a similar distance past the stands, passing through four more exceedingly fast bends to where the circuit turns right from the main road.

This corner is altogether sharper than the oasis turn and is followed by three relatively sharp bends, each about a quarter of a mile apart; in every case the bends are banked and perfectly surfaced. Once they are cleared, there follows a stretch of some two miles which would be absolutely straight except for three of the swinging curves which are a feature of the course. The road then turns again to the right, running straight back to the oasis, and through this to the grandstands.

Throughout the total lap distance of eight and a quarter miles, the circuit is very wide, and it had been specially treated before the race in order to make it as safe and as fast as possible. Palm trees dominate the road, rising between patches of sandy, arid ground, and lonely areas of country are visible where the back stretch runs down toward the sea.

The grandstand is a magnificent structure, built to provide the airiness essential to the temperature of Tripolitania; its cantilever roof can shelter over ten thousand spectators, although half again as many try to crowd into its shadow during the Grand Prix. In front of the stand is an enclosure raised above the level of the road, guarded by handrails set at the top of a stone wall. This wall—with the pits on the opposite side—places the starting point in what is almost a broad and shallow ravine, a situation duplicated on most of the bends and corners, where high safety banks are set both inside and outside the turns. The palm trees and the salt lake, the brilliant sunshine and the white-robed Arabs—who form a large proportion of the spectators— help to make the scene for the Grand Prix of Tripoli one without parallel.

Few other events are run off amidst such excitement, because the result of the race governs the distribution of prizes in a sweepstake, the existence of which has helped to lift the Grand Prix from comparative obscurity to an event of unusual importance. The fact that drivers receive a percentage of the total amount of this lottery helps to make the race formidable. The event itself carries a first prize of rather less than £700, but the percentage interest in the lottery brings this up to £6,000, with £4,000 for the second man home, and £3,000 for the driver who gains third place. These awards are scaled down to tenth place in the event, while there are prizes for the leader of the race at ten, twenty, and thirty laps.

Consolation prizes are also given to drivers who complete the first five laps within a certain time, and others for

those who cover the first two laps; this is designed to encourage drivers to keep their cars running as fast as possible, whatever the opening laps may bring in the way of mechanical difficulties.

As the authorities are particularly generous in the matter of starting fees, the Grand Prix offers compensation to every driver who takes part, no matter how indifferent may be his racing luck. The number of starters is,

*Air view of the Tripoli race track with one of the Indianapolis
cars coming past the stand.*

however, limited to thirty, and the race is open only to men
who have won a true Grand Prix or have held the Italian
Speed Championship, who have taken world's records or
have placed in an international speed event during the two
previous seasons. When the number of entries exceeds
thirty, the organizers select drivers in the order of their
qualification.

This selective process is similar to that which obtains

for the Indianapolis race, where the number of cars permitted to start is limited to almost the same figure. As, however, the authorities there have no similar event in which drivers can prove themselves, eliminating trials are instituted on the track itself. Such regulations insure the presence of only the finest drivers, whose natural rivalry insures the race being fought at very high speed.

The Grand Prix of Tripoli began to grow really fast with the event held in 1929, when the winner, Brilli Peri, set up 83.7 mph; he was killed during practice for the race the following year, when Borzacchini won at 91.5 mph. The event was not held again until 1933, when Achille Varzi won at 105.3 mph, gaining for Tripoli the distinction of holding the world's fastest road race.

It was expected that the race for 1934 would be very much faster, because nearly all the cars had been prepared under the new Grand Prix formula. It was significant, however, that there were no German drivers and no German cars among the entrants; they missed the race—definitely the most outstanding road event of the year—only because their machines were not fully prepared. Many rumors were current concerning these cars, and when they did appear they were to introduce an element of real drama into the season, and to alter completely all existing ideas of road-racing speeds.

As it was, however, the Tripoli race was confined to Italian-built Alfa Romeo and Maserati cars, two Bugattis from France and two quite unexpected entries from the United States, providing one of the very rare occasions when American drivers have competed outside their own country.* They could hardly have selected a race in which

* Up to that time (1934) only, of course (*Ed.*)

they would be ranged against keener opposition because, in so important an event, it was inevitable that the various Continental stables should come to the line in full force.

The Scuderia Ferrari entered five cars, all Alfa Romeos driven by Count Trossi, Achille Varzi, Guy Moll, Louis Chiron, and Raymond Tadini—who had set the pace in the Mille Miglia. Another Italian stable, known as the Gruppo san Giorgio, ran a Maserati driven by Biondetti, and two Alfa Romeos in the hands of Battaglia and Renato Balestrero. The Bugatti *equipe* started with Pierre Wimille and René Dreyfus, and there were entries from a stable organized by Whitney Straight. In addition, various independents were running, and they would have been led by Nuvolari had he not crashed during a race at Alessandria a short time before; he had received injuries which made it impossible for him to drive.

A Maserati had been specially prepared for Nuvolari to handle in the Tripoli race; this car had been acquired by Whitney Straight, and was to be driven by his teammate H. C. Hamilton. He had run in the International Trophy and had done a good deal of racing on the Continent, until this season always with MG cars; his driving had a quality which promised that he would probably become a rival to the best of Italian and French drivers. Whitney Straight's Maserati was running under America's colors; a regulation existed that all cars should carry the international racing colors of the countries from which the drivers themselves came.

In addition to Hamilton, England was represented by Captain G. E. T. Eyston, who had an Alfa Romeo. He was particularly well known for the long string of records which he had broken, and his successes, like Hamilton's, had been gained very largely with MG machines.

As an American, Whitney Straight was companioned by the two drivers from the States. One of these was Peter De Paolo, with a front-wheel-drive eight-cylinder Miller; the other was Lou Moore, who had a normal four-cylinder racing Miller.

Peter De Paolo had been the American national champion in 1925 and again in 1930, and had won the Indianapolis race. Lou Moore had been victorious in very many board and dirt track events, and in 1933 had finished third at Indianapolis. Each was a remarkably fine driver on the track, but neither had any real experience of road events, while their cars were evolved from racing experience in America. A good deal of interest was roused by their entries, which seemed likely to decide whether very specialized American machines could withstand a hard road race; and the Tripoli event was certain to be hard on both men and cars.

Nearly every driver who had run at Monaco was on the course, and old rivalries were renewed at the moment the circuit was open for practice. Chiron, Guy Moll, Tadini, and Achille Varzi all lapped in under four minutes, equivalent to speeds of over 120 mph; and as each of these drivers was a member of the Ferrari stable, their speeds set the pace for the rest. The American drivers were content to take matters relatively quietly, although De Paolo showed the possibilities of his car by covering the course at 112 mph.

In spite of the very high speeds, the whole of the practice period passed without accident, except that Freddy Zehender—in a Maserati—misjudged the turn at the Tagiura oasis and went off the road. He was not hurt, however, and his car was only slightly damaged. Phillippe Etancelin, in another Maserati, had engine trouble during practice, and his car was never restored to its proper tune for the race. Whitney Straight cracked the cylinder block of his car and, repairs being impossible, came to the line with only seven of his eight cylinders functioning.

There was a total of twenty-three starters, and the cars carried only even numbers, running from No. 2, Pierre Wimille in a Bugatti, to No. 60, Balestrero in an Alfa Romeo; the equivalent to a double thirteen—No. 26—was missed out altogether. An excited crowd gathered, nearly every spectator possessing a ticket in the sweepstake. The final draw for the lottery, however, was not made until a short while before the actual start, so that fortunate ticket holders would have no time in which to approach drivers and endeavor to come to an "arrangement"; it seemed possible that such efforts might be made in view of the fact that the winner of the sweepstake would receive well over fifty thousand pounds.

During the earlier years the Tripoli event had sometimes been marred either by immoderate heat or by winds which, whipping up the sand about the course, made matters difficult for drivers. Narrow sections of the circuit had existed, also, where the road was bordered by sand and stones, which were dangerous to machines pulling over in passing other cars; these sections had all been cleared away by the widening of the road for 1934. The weather proved to be relatively cool, although the sunshine was intensely bright.

The cars were lined up in rows, level with one end of the long grandstand, the leading machines being opposite the tall control tower set behind the pits. Italy's flag flut-

tered from a staff above the tower, and a hundred other
flags hung from long cords stretched between the summit
and the level of the road. Crowds pressed close to the handrails in front of the enclosures, in one of which stood ancient palms, growing from the bare earth and signifying
the spirit of Tripoli as they flung shadows across the road
in front of the cars.

The starter was Marshall Balbo, and the instant that
his flag fell, Piero Taruffi—who had raced against the MG
Magnettes in Italy—sent his sixteen-cylinder Maserati
into the lead, while the ranks of cars broke up behind him,
the machines accelerating fiercely down the road, raising dust that hung in the air long after they had raced
through the bend which lay immediately after the grandstand. While their furious roaring echoed backward, Chiron, Varzi, and Guy Moll—all the Ferrari stable—came
into position at Taruffi's tail; behind them Pierre Wimille
and Dreyfus drew their Bugattis out of the pack in pursuit of the Alfa Romeos.

The rest began to string out in the rush to the
first corner, but the leading cars remained close together,
bunching as they took the turn and running nose to tail
through the three bends which led to the back stretch.
They touched over 130 mph as they raced down it, to
corner again where the road ran between twin lakes, then
straightened for the corner by the oasis. Taruffi still held
the lead here, and he was still ahead when the machines
appeared at the end of the first lap.

As they shot along the sunken road between stands
and pits the howl of the Maserati sounded harshly, immediately to be lost in the high whine of the three Alfa Romeos which chased it. The four machines had covered that

first lap, from a standing start, at a speed very little below
120 mph; Taruffi was separated from Chiron by three-
fifths of a second, Varzi was one second further behind,
with Moll not more than a few feet in the rear. The following Bugattis were very near, their paintwork catching the
sunshine so that the machines flashed with a steely blue,
moving like screeching projectiles. They vanished into the
bend, and the rest came by, the two white Miller cars fighting against Alfa Romeos and Maseratis in the middle of
the string of machines.

The speed mounted during the second lap, and Taruffi increased his lead. Of the men so close behind him,
Chiron was the finest road-racing driver in the world. Varzi
was an Italian champion, and Guy Moll was proving himself to be their equal; Taruffi had yet to win a great race,
but he was setting a pace which was better than anything
the Ferrari men could achieve.

On the third lap he drew still further away. He
cleared the bend beyond the grandstands before Chiron
appeared on the straight behind. This was a warning to the
Frenchman, and he opened flat out over the fourth lap,
fearing that Taruffi might get too great a lead. Chiron
covered the course at a speed which set up a new record
for the race; when he passed the control tower again, time-
keepers saw that he had averaged 125.21 mph. In all the
history of motor racing no road circuit had ever been covered at so high a pace, and when Chiron had passed the
grandstand he was moving at very close to 160 mph. Even
this, however, was not fast enough to enable him to catch
Taruffi's Maserati, although he closed the gap which lay
between the two cars.

The fifth lap ran out, and again the leaders passed

the stands: Taruffi—Chiron—Varzi—Moll—the Bugattis—and then came Hamilton with his Maserati; ever since the start he had been shaking off cars in the howling pack which followed, getting into a position from which he might hope to challenge the Ferrari men. At the end of the sixth lap Hamilton was on the tail of the rearmost Bugatti. Farther back the two American drivers were riding close together, but they had already discovered that their brakes were inadequate for such a race as this; they had to cut out long before the Continental cars in order to slow sufficiently to get through the corners, and this meant loss of time.

With the start of the seventh circuit began the first of many changes in the race. Taruffi crashed disastrously on the corner at the end of the grandstand stretch. He was being pressed very closely by Chiron, and Varzi had opened up until he was only a few yards behind the French-

Whitney Straight's Maserati comes through the fast left-hand turn beyond the stand.

man. Trying to hold them off, Taruffi put his car too fast at the corner, and was unable to go through the turn.

His brakes screeched as he used them savagely, striving to cut down his speed, then came the scream of tires as the machine slid sideways in a tremendous skid, and moving at 100 mph, it shot completely off the road. The driver was flung from the cockpit as the car pitched sideways and smashed through a palisade, Taruffi himself being thrown to the ground just behind an ambulance which stood clear of the turn. The attendants rendered first aid as he lay there, then rushed him to hospital; he was severely injured, but made a remarkable recovery and was ready to race again before the season ended.

This crash gave Chiron the lead, and it was now that Hamilton opened out. He passed Dreyfus, went by Wimille, then set himself to challenge the Alfa Romeos that lay ahead. In three laps more he overtook Guy Moll, dueling with him all along the back stretch, and passing him as the machines came out of the oasis corner. Only Chiron and Varzi were in front of Hamilton now, but Guy Moll was clinging to his tail, waiting for a chance to regain the place that he had lost. The machines remained in this order until the fifteenth lap, then Chiron paid the penalty of his hard driving; the tread began to break up on a tire, forcing him to stop at his pit. In the grandstand excited spectators stood up to watch him make a fast wheel change, others pressed to the rails by the enclosures, while all around the course the crowds stared blankly when they saw that Chiron was missing.

For the second time the leadership of the race changed. Varzi automatically took the place which Chiron had held, and this made Hamilton, now in second place, a danger to the dominant position of the Scuderia Ferrari. Guy Moll, riding behind him, knew this, and it was a matter of team tactics that he should do his utmost to pass Hamilton and so place himself ready to back up Varzi's efforts.

Moll used full throttle as they left the grandstand behind, coming to Hamilton's tail when they cornered past the wreckage of Taruffi's machine. The two fought it out along the back stretch, and this time the Alfa Romeo driver was ahead when they came away from the oasis, gaining for the Ferrari stable first and second places, with Hamilton a close third.

He was the only English driver who was doing at all well; Eyston had broken a piston, but was continuing the race with only seven of his Alfa Romeo's cylinders functioning. Other drivers were having trouble. Dreyfus slowed, making the first of several calls at his pit, while Whitney Straight had retired on the eleventh lap.

Chiron came into the race again, after the briefest of delays at his pit. Short though his stop had been, it was enough to put him among the pack which chased the leaders, and he required four laps before he could draw ahead and come in sight of Wimille, who was running in fourth place. All this time Hamilton and Moll had been traveling close together, and it was as Chiron passed Wimille that Hamilton slipped in front of Moll, riding second to Varzi once again; he deserved his position, because his driving was very impressive and he handled his machine with a cool skill which matched that of Varzi himself.

Just after the twentieth lap—half distance—Chiron closed down on Moll. In one lap more he had passed him and began to chase Hamilton, with Moll struggling to regain the place he had lost. For nearly the whole of a lap these three cars went around in very close company, moving at a little below the record speed which the Frenchman had already established. In front was the flying Varzi, cornering with a precision and certainty which matched the mechanical efficiency of his machine.

Now that half the race had been run the cars were dust-smirched, and the drivers were visible as stiff, goggled figures which became active only in the corners when, at times, they had to fight to hold their machines. No road race had ever been run off at so high a speed as this, and the strain was shown by the way in which some machines constantly drew up at their pits for attention and by the lengthening list of retirements. The interest of the crowd centered on Chiron as he tried to pass Hamilton, with Moll clinging the while to Chiron's tail. The Frenchman had the greater speed, and presently he went ahead, then drove all out after Varzi. He could not catch him, and until the thirtieth lap the race continued with Varzi—Chiron—Hamilton—Moll—Wimille—holding the positions they had gained.

During all those long laps the issue of the race was held in suspense. Each driver among the leaders was trying to wear his rivals down, and no one could guess what the outcome might be, because the five machines were separated by seconds only. Then suddenly Wimille slowed, dropped back, and stopped at his pit with a broken oil pipe which made it impossible for him to continue. The other four went on until Hamilton's engine appeared to give under the strain; it began to misfire and he fell away, when Moll roared triumphantly past him. With his exhaust note changed to a broken, blurred thudding, Hamilton drew to

The two Alfa-Romeos at the finish line
Varzi wins from Moll by about four feet.

the side of the road and ran on to his pit, there to retire from the race through ignition trouble.

These two were not alone in misfortune. The tremendous pace on that arid circuit had eliminated nearly half the starters, and with only ten more laps to cover it seemed the event was virtually over and that the result lay between Varzi and Chiron—but Guy Moll had been holding a little speed in hand.

Varzi was some fifteen seconds in front of the Frenchman, and Chiron was separated by about the same distance from Moll, who now began to close in and to do it more rapidly than Chiron was gaining on Varzi. Each time that the cars came around at the end of a lap, Chiron was nearer the leader, but Moll was still closer to Chiron.

Five laps from the end, real drama entered the race. Moll came to Chiron's tail, and it was obvious that he would pass, while calculations showed that the young Frenchman might yet catch Varzi himself. When they came around again, Moll was in front of Chiron, who was striving desperately to hold him. He could not do it. The space between the two widened—and it narrowed between Moll and the leader.

Varzi knew that his position was threatened. He drove with his throttle pedal hard down, handling his machine with all the skill and courage that his great experience had given him. The young Frenchman matched this with natural flair and ability, beating all that Varzi could do, gaining ground steadily, again and again placing his car in readiness to pass but never quite achieving it.

When Varzi appeared along the grandstand stretch to enter the final lap, Moll was only a few yards behind him. The two machines flashed past and, five seconds afterwards, Chiron came by. Less than six seconds separated the three machines, even though they had covered much more than three hundred miles and had been racing for over two and a half hours. It was obvious that anything might happen before the three came around again.

The result of the Tripoli sweepstake was thus in doubt as the last lap began. When the cars had gone by they left behind agitated spectators in the grandstand, and enclosures filled with onlookers whose excitement was duplicated all around the circuit. Moll cut down Varzi's one-second lead along the falling stretch where the road ran toward Tripoli, but he gained nothing on the bends beyond the corner. He drew still closer to Varzi as they raced at the back of the course, and the cars were all but wheel to wheel when they came from the oasis turn.

Down the straightaway Varzi still led, but by no more than four times the length of his own car. Both traveled absolutely flat out toward the finishing line, with Moll holding his Alfa Romeo to one side of the road, clear of the grit and dust kicked back by the leading car and in a position to pass. But he did not pass. He could not find sufficient speed, and Varzi crossed the line with a lead of just one-fifth of a second.

Varzi's average was 116.3 mph, his time for the total distance of 327.5 miles being 2 hr. 48 min. 53 sec. With Guy Moll in second place, Chiron came home third, and the man in fourth place was Etancelin, who finished 6 min. 44 sec. behind Varzi. He was followed by Dreyfus, Biondetti, then by Peter De Paolo, Lou Moore, and Eyston. These nine drivers were the only men to complete the course.

GRAND PRIX, *1935*

TRIPOLI GRAND PRIX 1934 RESULTS		
1ST	A. Varzi	Alfa Romeo 116.3 mph average
2ND	G. Moll	Alfa Romeo
3RD	L. Chiron	Alfa Romeo

CHAPTER SIX:

Until the American Indianapolis drivers brought their track cars to Italy in 1957 and 1958, the fastest race ever run in the world took place in Germany in May, 1937. The 1937 Avusrennen remains to this day the fastest race ever to be won by a road-racing car, and the speed of the winner, Hermann Lang, has never been exceeded by any other European driver.

When Adolph Hitler established his Nazi dictatorship in Germany in 1933, one of his aims was to show the world

FASTEST IN EUROPE –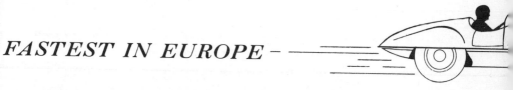

the superiority of German technical ability. German designers built some of the finest roads, fighting aircraft, tanks, and guns. Hitler also offered large amounts of money to manufacturers in order that Germany should break the supremacy of Italy and France in Grand Prix racing. Thanks to the technicians of the Mercedes-Benz and Auto-Union factories, Germany soon possessed the finest and fastest racing machines in the world. By the middle of the 1934 road-racing season in Europe, they had proved their superiority over the contemporary Bugattis and Alfa Romeos and Maseratis. From then until the outbreak of World War II in 1939, only the Alfa Romeo in the hands of that ace driver Tazio Nuvolari was able on rare occasions to break the string of German victories.

During these years the world saw some of the most closely fought and exciting road races ever to take place. The cars were giants of cars—faster and more powerful than any built since; the men were giants of men, with the physical strength of the early great drivers combined with finesse and razor-sharp reactions and perception. One of these drivers, when asked what it was like driving a 600-horsepower racing car on a winding road circuit, could compare the experience only with riding a 500-cc. motor bike on ice, in a hurry and in a strong cross-wind!

Of the Mercedes-Benz and Auto-Union, the W125 Mercedes-Benz was slightly the more powerful. It had a straight-eight engine with a bore of 94 mm. and a stroke of 102 mm., and a total cubic capacity of 5,660 cc.—no greater than that of many American passenger cars of today. But besides weighing less than half the weight of an average American sedan and having a very small frontal area, the Mercedes possessed an engine of great refinement

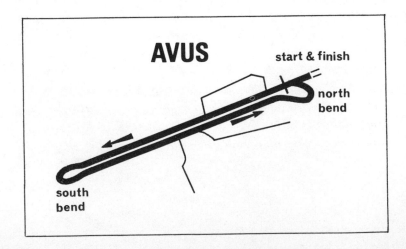

and complexity. Two overhead camshafts operated four valves per cylinder, and the cylinder block was made up of forged steel barrels welded together in sets of four. Other expensive items included split roller-type main and big end bearings, a most elaborate cooling system with corrugated water jackets for differential expansion, and hollow exhaust valves. A supercharger, with a boost pressure of up to 12 lbs. per sq. in., was included in the specification and helped to raise the maximum power output to some 650 hp at 5,800 rpm.

The Auto-Union, the strangest and most unlovely racing car ever built, was little less powerful, and could easily exceed a speed of 200 mph. It was a rear-engined machine with a short stubby nose, and was a very dangerous car until you learned how to master it. Only two drivers ever succeeded in doing: Bernd Rosemeyer, the young German hero, and Nuvolari, who switched his allegiance from Alfa Romeo when he discovered that even his uncanny genius at the wheel could not bring the Italian car the checkered flag. The designer was the notable Austrian engineer Dr. Ferdinand Porsche, who was also responsible for the big Mercedes sports cars of the 1920s, the Volkswagen which we know so well today, and the notorious Tiger tank. It had a V16 engine of even greater complexity than that of the Mercedes.

A special breed of driver had to be sought out and trained to drive these elaborate projectiles. Among the most famous was Rudolf Caracciola, a boyish-looking veteran by 1937 and the greatest driver in the world at that time, after Nuvolari. Count Manfred von Brauchitsch was a proud aristocrat who took defeat as a personal slight. Then there were Hans von Stuck, unbeatable at hill climbs, the British champion Dick Seaman, Rosemeyer the gay playboy, Hermann Lang the serious professional, von Delius, and several others.

In May, 1937, cars and drivers converged on the fastest track circuit in the world, the Avus ring on the outskirts of Berlin. Half the city came out to watch, for word had got around that this was likely to be the fastest motor race ever run. It was a bright day and the bands were playing and the flags were fluttering. The scene must have resembled quite closely a champion chariot race at the height of the Roman Empire; but the noise was greater, and the speeds, you will see from this contemporary account, were greatly higher!

THE CHIEF CONTESTANTS	
DRIVERS	CARS
Rudolf Caracciola (Germany)	Mercedes-Benz 5.7 liters
Richard Seaman (Britain)	Mercedes-Benz 5.7 liters
Manfred von Brauchitsch (Germany)	Mercedes-Benz 5.7 liters
Hermann Lang (Germany)	Mercedes-Benz 5.7 liters
Bernd Rosemeyer (Germany)	Auto-Union 6 liters
Ernst Hasse (Germany)	Auto-Union 6 liters
Ernst von Delius (Germany)	Auto-Union 6 liters
(all cars German)	

BY "GRANDE VITESSE"

A crowd of 380,000 people thronged the enclosure surrounding the Avus toll road in Berlin last Sunday afternoon to watch the first race meeting held there since the building of the almost vertical banking of the north turn. There was no race last year. Hundreds of thousands of spectators had to be turned away from the gates. Dr. Goebbels, minister of propaganda under the Nazi regime, and many other high personages were present, and before the start, Sport Leader Huhnlein welcomed the competitors.

The sun beat down mercilessly on the huge crowds and the race was run in great heat, which must have proved exhausting to the drivers, handling their cars at hitherto unheard-of speeds.

After their disappointment at Tripoli the Ferrari Alfas were nonstarters in this super-race at which speeds of over 200 mph were seen on the 6-mile straights of this course which runs up and down in parallel lines, divided only by a grass margin, and is joined at the south end by a gently banked sweep and at the north by the new "Wall of Death" with its brick surfacing and slope of about 1 in 1.

A crowd of no fewer than 40,000 paid for admission to the enclosure overlooking this astonishing banking. All were on tiptoe with enthusiasm.

Rosemeyer was in the super streamlined record-breaking Auto-Union, but without the coupe top, Delius in an ordinary Grand Prix Auto-Union, Rudolf Caracciola drove a normal Grand Prix Mercedes, Seaman the same, Balestrero was the only Italian representative with a 3-liter six-cylinder Alfa Romeo. Freddy Zehender (Mercedes) was a nonstarter.

The start was stupendous, and instantly Delius, with terrific acceleration and tires smoking, shot into the lead, with Dick Seaman grimly on his tail and Rosemeyer a bad third.

On the next lap Rosemeyer put his well-known foot hard down and tore past both of them. Delius tried to pass again on the north banking and frightened 40,000 Germans out of their wits, but Rosemeyer drew away.

On lap three the order was Rosemeyer, Delius, Seaman (a close third), and Caracciola fourth. On lap four Caracciola opened out and passed Seaman, who strained every nerve to repass the great Rudolf, but couldn't quite make it. Then Caracciola passed Delius and went hell for leather after Rosemeyer. Both cars screamed around the north wall almost level, one above the other—a terrifying

*The start of the 1937 Avusrennen.
The Auto-Union in the center has
standard road-racing body.*

MERCEDES-BENZ PHOTO

sight—and Seaman fell back a little. But on the sixth lap all four cars were on the north banking together—one of the most staggering sights to be seen in modern motor racing. Balestrero ran fifth, a lap behind the rest.

Rosemeyer's lap of 172.75 mph was the fastest in the race, but Caracciola was only fractionally slower. Caracciola opened the throttle wide on the last few miles, held the car to the north wall by main force and snatched past Rosemeyer as they swept round to finish, and won by a matter of seconds.

Caracciola took 32 min. 29.6 sec. for the seven laps, a speed of 155.598 mph. Seaman in fourth place behind von Delius (Auto-Union) took only 32 min. 48.6 sec., averaging 154.044 mph, and was warmly acclaimed by the crowd.

The second heat brought out Fagioli, driving for Auto-Unions this year (Mercedes last year) and winner of the last Avusrennen in 1935 at 148.20 mph (when Stuck put up the record lap for Auto-Unions at 161.88 mph).

*Caracciola's streamlined Mercedes-Benz being
wheeled out for the start.*

MERCEDES-BENZ PHOTO

The Italian was driving a super-streamlined Auto-Union;
Hasse (Auto-Union) had an open Grand Prix car. Von
Brauchitsch (Mercedes) had the new 12-cylinder car with
streamlined body but open wheels. Land, victor at Tripoli, drove a normal G.P. Mercedes. Cholmondeley Tapper
(Maserati) was a nonstarter. Hartmann and Soffietti
drove 6-cylinder Maseratis.

On the first lap Fagioli led by a couple of lengths from
Lang, who seemed to be repeating his Tripoli form. Close
behind roared Hasse, then Brauchitsch and Hartmann,

*Above, it enters the north bend,
banking at full throttle.*

MERCEDES-BENZ PHOTO

who both frightened the crowds with their angles on the north wall.

Then Brauchitsch went past all three leaders in one stupendous rush, Lang running second now. Soffietti was already a lap behind in three laps, a few yards ahead of Lang, but that worthy burst a tire on the fifth lap and lost ground, despite a lightning change, leaving Brauchitsch to lead by a long gap from Hasse.

On the last lap Brauchitsch eased up and won comfortably with Hasse second, Lang third, and Hartmann

(On the following pages)
*Caracciola takes his Mercedes-Benz high on the north bend,
banking to overtake Rosemeyer's Auto-Union.
Both cars were specially streamlined for this race.*

MERCEDES-BENZ PHOTO

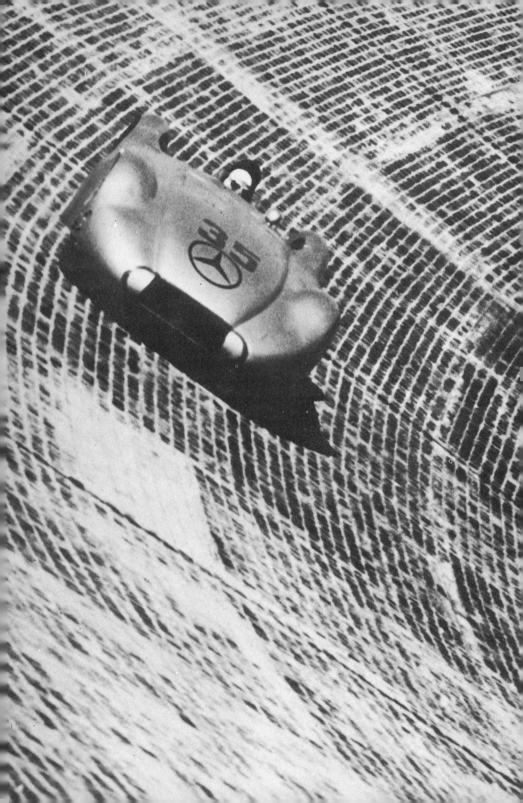

fourth. Lang did the fastest lap at 171.630 mph.

Then came the final. So far there had been little tire trouble (both Auto-Unions and Mercedes were running on colossal diameter rear wheels) so that the final was expected to be the same.

The starters were Caracciola, Delius, Seaman, Brauchitsch, Hasse, Lang, and Hartmann. Hasse had to yield his good starting position to Lang, as it was averred that Hasse had balked Lang on the north wall.

Caracciola shot into the lead on lap one, shaking Delius off his tail through the south curve. Seaman ran third, but was passed by Lang. Brauchitsch retired after the first lap.

On the third lap the order round the south curve was Caracciola, Lang, and Seaman—all Mercedes.

On the fourth round came a sensation—Caracciola

Close combat at the south bend, with von Brauchitsch just holding off Lang (car 37) and Delius.

MERCEDES-BENZ PHOTO

blew up, and the order became Lang, Delius (Auto-Union), Hasse (Auto-Union), and Seaman (Mercedes).

Lang extended his lead, while Seaman fell back to fifth place. The race now became a terrific struggle between Lang, Delius, and Hasse. Both Rosemeyer and Seaman appeared to have slowed up. Then suddenly Seaman spurted and passed Rosemeyer on the south curve, and the best Rosemeyer could do in reply was to get his car half a length in front of Seaman's.

No one could challenge Lang, and that newcomer to the limelight of racing scored his second win for Mercedes with a time of 35 min. 30.4 sec. Behind him the order was Delius, Hasse, and Rosemeyer (Auto-Unions), with Seaman fifth in 36 min. 50.4 sec.

The fastest lap was Caracciola's 4 min. 33.4 sec. (162.061 mph).

THE MOTOR *June 1, 1937*

AVUSRENNEN 1937 RESULTS		
1ST	Hermann Lang	Mercedes-Benz 162.62 mph average
2ND	Ernst von Delius	Auto-Union
3RD	Ernst Hasse	Auto-Union

CHAPTER SEVEN:

An auto race as famous in Britain as America's Indianapolis 500 was the Brooklands 500. Of course today the Indy speeds are far higher than those of any race run at Brooklands. But in the 1920s and 1930s, the British Racing Drivers' Club's 500-mile race was the fastest long-distance event in the world. Later, as you will see from this

120

FASTEST AROUND
BROOKLANDS

account by *William Boddy, author of* The History of Brooklands Motor Course *and editor of the magazine* Motor Sport, *the distance was reduced to 500 kilometers, and the speed went up accordingly. As a consequence, the 1937 event became the fastest race ever run around the concrete saucer.*

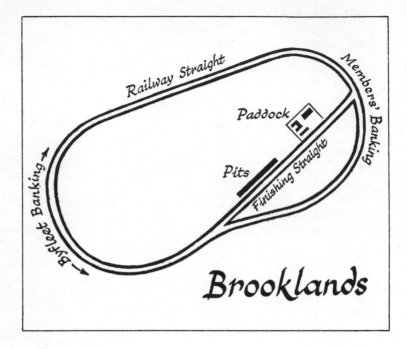

THE CHIEF CONTESTANTS	
DRIVERS	CARS
J. Cobb (Britain)	Napier-Railton 24 liters (Britain)
B. Bira (Siam)	Delahaye 4 liters (France)
G. Duller (Britain)	Duesenberg 6.9 liters (U.S.A.)
A. Dobson (Britain)	Riley 2 liters (Britain)

BY WILLIAM BODDY

British officialdom has never been very enthusiastic about motor racing, or motoring for that matter, and no one has succeeded in making it legal to close English roads temporarily for the purpose of running speed contests over them.

What can be done in this direction in Europe is an offense in England, although permitted on occasions in Jersey, Ireland, and the Isle of Man. It was due to this overcautious attitude that England gained the distinction of having the world's first motor course at Brooklands in Surrey.

This unique pioneer track, a giant 2¾-mile oval with two of its turns steeply banked, was built, very quickly, between the fall of 1906 and the summer of 1907 —using wild Irish labor sheltered at night in one communal hut—by the late Hugh Fortesque Locke King at a cost to him of some 150,000 sovereigns.

Brooklands Motor Course became one of the minor wonders of the world, a magnet for Edwardian society and the mechanically minded, when it was declared open in July, 1907. It has gone the way of so many symbols of those leisurely pre-1914 days and of the mad twenties that followed. Yet it remains remarkable, not only on account of the immense, intense amount of automobile and aeronautical history that was enacted within the shelter of its concrete slopes, but because of the foresight shown by those engineers and contractors responsible for it.

Brooklands was remarkably well equipped for its day. Tunnels and bridges simplified the movement of spectators and officials, there were admirable restaurants, concrete garages and electric timing apparatus for all competitors, together with a magnificent clubhouse. For more social occasions there were tennis courts and cafes, and if you wanted to fly in for an afternoon's racing, you could always use the airfield in the center of the track.

That was Brooklands. That was how true-blue enthusiasts liked their motor racing from 1907 to 1939. Present-day circuits may attract far bigger crowds and make a profit. The very reason that the late-lamented Brooklands track scarcely paid its way was, in my opinion, very largely due to its immensity and the lavish scale on which it was conducted—as a veritable gentleman's estate, necessitating full-time gardeners, painters, carpenters, and gatekeepers for its upkeep. Oh, dignified, thorough, glamorous age, long since departed!

At first, racing at the new motor course was very much in the Ascot and Goodwood (horse) tradition. The drivers wore their entrants' colors in the form of smocks and caps. Entry fees and prizes were declared in sovereigns, and the contests were given picturesque names such as the Marcel Renault Memorial Plate or the Gottlieb Daimler Memorial Plate. Prize money, incidentally, was not ungenerous; it totaled nearly £5,000 at the initial meeting.

Thus with the roads of England out of bounds to racing cars, the sport flourished at Brooklands, which became the mecca of leather-coated, tweed-capped motoring enthusiasts who were keen on all aspects of making cars and motorcycles go far faster than their makers intended.

Some people hold that the vast expanses of the track were wasted. They would have liked long-distance, Grand-

Prix-style races to have been run there regularly, and earlier use of artificial corners, which were not laid out at Brooklands until 1925. Long-distance races were infrequent at Brooklands. From the earliest days the fastest cars—and they could attain 120 mph by 1908—contested the O'Gorman Trophy, originally over a distance of about 100 miles but by 1909 substantially shortened.

There were some long-duration stock-car contests prior to the outbreak of World War I. Otherwise, short races were the fashion. True, in 1921 the motorcyclists showed the way with a remarkable 500-mile race. It was never repeated. That year, too, the ambitious Junior Car Club staged the first of its 200-mile races, all the more remarkable in that they were restricted to 1,100 and 1,500-cc. cars at a time when light cars were in a still primitive state of development.

It was not until 1929 that another 500-mile race was held at Brooklands; it was for cars and was run around the outer circuit with no artificial corners, so that the emphasis was on flat-out speed. It was destined to become the fastest long-distance motor race in the world, being won in its heyday at a higher average speed than the famous Indianapolis 500-mile race in America. In its final form it was the fastest race of this length ever held in England.

The club responsible for this daring and destructive contest was the British Racing Drivers' Club, formed at the suggestion of a few British "speed kings" in 1928 to keep a watching brief on matters affecting the pleasure, health, and well-being of racing drivers and racing motorists (to my mind there is a subtle distinction between the two, which is unimportant in the present context). The B.R.D.C. is now a very important organization, with

H.R.H. The Duke of Edinburgh as its president-in-chief. The beauty of the club in its early days was that every member was required to have accomplished certain achievements at the wheel of a racing car; this is still substantially true, but the B.R.D.C. is bigger now and has attracted a number of nonracing honorary members. However, I digress....

Having formed itself, the B.R.D.C. considered that it should organize a race for its members. It finally decided that a good long blind round-and-round Brooklands track was the thing best suited to their temperaments and the diverse kinds of cars they could muster.

In this fashion the first B.R.D.C. 500-mile race came into being. It was run in October, 1929, when the racing season was nearing its end, so that if competing cars "blew up" there would be time during the winter in which to repair the havoc. In order to permit a diverse collection of racing cars—from ancient Grand Prix machines and home-built specials to stripped sports cars and modern confections—to compete together amicably, the contest was a handicap affair. About this time there was no particular difficulty, because Brooklands was the home of the individual handicap, and the performance of the cars could be assessed to a nicety. In fact, the "500" was more of a gamble, for it was handicapped in capacity classes.

This first B.R.D.C. 500-mile race attracted a remarkable field, ranging from Austin 7s to monster Bentleys, which was to become traditional. It was a fine race, won at 107.32 mph by Frank Clement and Jack Barclay in a nonsupercharged 4½-liter Bentley, after a hair-raising skidding ride. Clive Dunfee and Sammy Davis were second in a 6½-liter Bentley, and a third place was secured by

Cyril Paul and John Cobb in a Sunbeam.

Thereafter this great race became an annual end-of-the-season frolic at Brooklands. It embraced humor and tragedy, and took tremendous toll of the starters as it progressed throughout the long autumnal afternoons in thin sunshine or torrential rain. I recall sitting in the wooden pits at the Fork listening carefully to the exhaust note of each car as it passed, wondering whether this would be a race *sans* finishers. Of course, it never was. . . .

The 1930 "500" was a victory for the Earl of March and Sammy Davis, in a small blood-orange Austin 7 at 83.42 mph. Second and third places were taken by Benjafield and Hall, in a Bentley, and Purdy and Cushman, in a Sunbeam. The following year the race was won by Jack Dunfee and Cyril Paul, in a Bentley. They averaged 118.39 mph and led home the Hon. Brian Lewis and Saunders-Davies, in a Talbot, and Eddie Hall, in his MG. Ron Horton and Jack Bartlett won the 1932 race in an MG at 96.29 mph, and Hall's MG took the 1933 event at 106.53 mph. The irrepressible Freddy Dixon, in a Riley, was the 1934 victor at 104.8 mph. By 1935 John Cobb had his special-track Napier-Railton on form, winning at the record speed of 121.28 mph. In 1936 Dixon and Charlie Martin brought a Riley home in first place at 116.86 mph.

Now this 500-mile race was very tough on cars. By 1937 Brooklands was rough and bumpy—its scars never really healed from the World War I period, when R.F.C. lorries used to trundle around it. Unkind critics said it was debatable which suffered more, the cars or the track, during the "500."

So for 1937 the B.R.D.C., in its wisdom, decided to

John Cobb in his Napier-Railton high on the Brooklands' banking.

reduce the length of its race without spoiling the title. The 500-mile race became the 500-kilometer race, and has gone down in history as England's fastest long-distance contest.

The date was September 18, the distance 112 laps, and handicapping was now on a system of credit laps, so that only the bigger, tougher cars had the full 500 kilometers to cover. The entry list was fully up to expectations, but practice was marred by Parnell's MG sliding down the banking onto Mrs. Petre's Austin 7, inflicting injuries on this attractive and superbly courageous lady driver from which she has never quite recovered.

The real excitement of this particular race was watching the big fellows lapping at over 120 mph at the rim of the Brooklands' bankings, overtaking smaller cars for which they were unable to brake, their tires the criterion between a safe run and almost certain disaster. Brave, these drivers of "heavy metal," prepared to go on and on for hour after hour.

Unfortunately two of these cars, the Barnato-Hassan and the Bentley-Jackson, together with Continental entries such as the Talbots and V12 Delahayes, were nonstarters. Consequently most eyes were on John Cobb's huge 24-liter Napier-Railton, winner in 1935, a specially built track car contrived round an old Napier "Lion" aeroengine to take the world's 24-hour record, which it did at Utah, U.S.A., in 1936 at 150.6 mph. It had a heavy chassis with double cantilever back springs and incorporated some beautiful machine-shop work by the Thomson and Taylor Brooklands' workshops, as you will appreciate if you go and look at it in the Montagu Motor Museum.

A tricky wind prevailed during the race and the enormous tires on the big car had to be observed very carefully, but Cobb, with Oliver Bertram as his intrepid co-driver, found it possible to keep to the prearranged race plan. There was opposition in the form of Austin Dobson's fearsome twin-engined Alfa Romeo, but its fuel tank worked loose and delayed it.

At 3 P.M. on that dramatic afternoon two Rileys,

Arthur Dobson's and Cyril Paul's, led from the Napier-Railton. Hadley's Austin had broken a piston, the Bentley-engined Bowler-Hofman suffered similar trouble, and a Maserati's fuel tank punctured. Half an hour later Cobb swept into the lead, averaging 129.4 mph. Prince Bira was going splendidly in his stripped sports car Delahaye until acid from the battery attacked his arm. Duller's American Duesenberg, which could have challenged Cobb, had clutch slip, and troubles were rife in most pits.

The Napier-Railton was difficult to hold in the wind, but survived a deflation of a back tire. The wheels were heavy and pit stops serious; this one occupied three minutes. Nevertheless, the big car was formidable when it was going, lapping at some 130 mph. Other cars stopped, resumed, or retired. Goodacre had a narrow escape when his Austin's steering track-rod broke. But the Napier-Railton, its 12-cylinder aeroengine hardly extended, went on and on. A routine tire change and refueling stop cost it 1½ minutes and it was below handicap. But it led, two Rileys behind it. Nothing now could snatch victory from Cobb except a mechanical failure, and the Napier-Railton was essentially durable. It ran on to receive the checkered flag, having averaged 127.05 mph, winner of England's fastest long-distance race. The big car had been in action for 2 hr. 26 min. 24.4 sec. It did its last lap at 136.45 mph and I recall seeing it pass the finishing line with one of its tire treads flapping around the wheel, a dramatic finish because few of the spectators knew that Cobb had been flagged home. Dobson's 2-liter Riley was second, Maclure's smaller Riley third.

Earl Howe presented Cobb and Bertram with their victors' plaques; Ken Taylor, who was largely responsible for the car, was towed away sitting happily at the wheel; the last B.R.D.C. "500," a high-speed race between typically British cars over a banked track, was over.

We shall never see its like again. . . .

W. Boddy is the Brooklands historian
and acknowledged authority on the track.
He contributed this account
at the editor's request.

BROOKLANDS 500 KM. 1937 RESULTS		
1ST	J. Cobb	Napier-Railton 127.05 mph average
2ND	A. Dobson	Riley
3RD	C. Paul	Riley

CHAPTER EIGHT:

Even today, when the French nation possesses no racing or sports cars or even drivers of great importance, no one would dispute the French claim that their 24-hour Grand Prix d'Endurance at Le Mans is the greatest annual motoring event. "Everyone," they say, "comes to Le Mans." Certainly a sports car manufacturer intent on establishing or maintaining his reputation in the industry must come to Le Mans sooner or later to prove to the world the speed and reliability of his products in the toughest auto racing

FASTEST SOLO RUN

grind of them all. And the Sarthe circuit draws more spectators from more nations than any other auto race; although, if the truth be known, it is, without exception, also the dullest motor race to watch after the first few hours.

Le Mans was never designed as a public spectacle, and the authorities from the very first event in 1923 saw to it that there were enough sideshows to keep the paying customers amused after they had become dizzy and bored staring at the sports cars rushing past them. Le Mans was

*designed to test the sheer endurance of cars and drivers:
to work away, hour after hour. through an afternoon, an
evening, a night, a morning, and half another afternoon,
and seek out the mechanical frailties of the machines and
the human frailties of the men driving them. To share the
driving seat with another at Le Mans makes tremendous
demands on the physical and mental capacity of a man.*

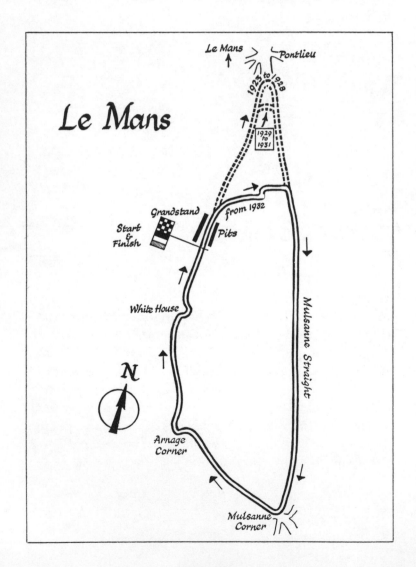

To drive a heavy, high-powered sports car through daylight and darkness, and the treacherous dawn mist for which Le Mans is notorious—alone for the full twenty-four hours—borders on madness or on a degree of courage that few of us can expect to understand.

This is a story of a brave Frenchman, Pierre Levegh, who attempted the near-impossible—to drive the full Le Mans without assistance, in the fastest car in the race, and win against the full works teams of great sports car manufacturers like Jaguar, Aston Martin, Mercedes-Benz, and Ferrari.

THE CHIEF CONTESTANTS	
DRIVERS	CARS
P. Levegh (*France*)	Talbot 4.5 liters (*France*)
J. Behra (*France*) R. Manzon (*France*)	Gordini 2.3 liters (*France*)
J. Fitch (*U.S.A.*) H. Rice (*U.S.A.*)	Cunningham 5.4 liters (*U.S.A.*)
B. Cunningham (*U.S.A.*) W. Spear (*U.S.A.*)	Cunningham 5.4 liters (*U.S.A.*)
P. Collins (*Britain*) L. Macklin (*Britain*)	Aston Martin 2.6 liters (*Britain*)
L. Johnson (*Britain*) T. Wisdom (*Britain*)	Nash-Healey 4.1 liters (*Britain*)
H. Lang (*Germany*) F. Reiss (*Germany*)	Mercedes-Benz 2.9 liters (*Germany*)
G. Helfrich (*Germany*) H. Niedermayer (*Germany*)	Mercedes-Benz 2.9 liters (*Germany*)
E. Chaboud (*France*) C. Pozzi (*France*)	Talbot 4.5 liters (*France*)

All this week the capital of the west of France, the ancient city of Le Mans, where Wilbur Wright was the first man to fly in Europe (from the aerodrome behind what are now the grandstand enclosures) has woken from its gentle provincial tranquility and become the focus of world interest in automobilism. Day by day the teams descended on the old town from Great Britain, Germany, Italy, America, as well as from France, and the famous Café Gruber on the Place de la République rang nightly with the voices of many nations. The car parks were packed with the cars of all countries. One saw the Aston Martins of Prince Bertil of Sweden parked alongside the Humber of Mr. Wilfred Andrews, chairman of the Royal Automobile Club who was to start the race, a gesture to the winning nation (Jaguar car) of last year.

Practicing from just before dusk to 1 A.M. each evening passed off with little incident, but with the usual alarm and despondency here and there. One Mercedes went off the road, an Aston Martin landed in a sandbank, and a Cunningham had to be bent back into shape. The lap times were remarkable. The Ferrari, Mercedes-Benz, and the 2.3 Gordini all got up to the Jaguar's lap record of last year (105.24 mph), and although there is no official timing, we were left with the news that Ascari in the 2.9-liter Ferrari saloon, driven by Bracco when winning the Mille Miglia, had circulated in 4 min. 21.6 sec., which on this 8.38-mile circuit with its long Mulsanne straight is 106.65 mph. The "Mercs," which shook us all by their speed, as in the Mille

Pierre Levegh before the start at the pits.
KLEMANTASKI PHOTO

Miglia and at Berne, had averaged around 4 min. 45 sec.
Simon's Ferrari about the same speed, Rosier's similar
vehicle three seconds slower, and Moss's Jaguar in 4 min.
43 sec.

This year the XK120C Jaguars appeared with re-
cently designed and remodeled bodies, having the fashion-
able plunging neckline to the hood and shorter tails. There

was worry in practice on account of heating, due, it was thought, to moving the water header tanks to a position behind the engine. This was altered for the race except on the Whitehead-Stewart car, but there was anxiety about the blocks and gaskets. One of the DB3 Aston Martins (Parnell) had a new coupe streamlined top with perspex windows and all three of these cars used the 1951 2.6-liter engines instead of the 2.9 liters tested experimentally at Monaco the other week. One of the Mercedes-Benz appeared with a futuristic rooftop air brake like a small aero wing for use on braking after the Mulsanne rush, but this was not used in the race. The Cunninghams surprisingly had flat, bus-type steering wheels. Chambas's Talbot had a supercharger and so did Constantin's Peugeot.

After days of desultory thunderstorms and heavy rain squalls, race day was heavily overcast, humid but cooled by a breeze. Half an hour before the start at 4 P.M. the cars began to start up and move to their positions, tail-on to the pits, for the classic Le Mans start in which the drivers race to their machines, jump in, press the starters and get going for twenty-four hours. The long line of pits—almost half a mile of them—was a colorful kaleidoscope of packed thousands, the counters crowded, the gallery overhead bulging with spectators. The enclosures were sardine packed. It was estimated 100,000 cars and 400,000 people had thronged to the circuit for this battle of the nations. Flags flew, programs waved, the restaurants and buvettes roared with the thunder of excited masses. The

The tense last seconds before the Le Mans start.
MERCEDES-BENZ PHOTO

minutes ticked away. Police chased the unwanted from the track, photographers had their usual violent arguments, drivers grew momentarily more nervous, chart keepers bent to their boards. Four o'clock approached. Tension could be felt even in our press stand.

Came the familiar hush, the tense silence as the drivers stood waiting on the opposite side of the road, then the flag dropped. Came the scamper of feet, then the whirring of starters, and the race for twenty-four hours had begun. Stirling Moss (Jaguar) moved first but far down the line was soon in the midst of the traffic. First around the bend and out of sight raced Fitch (Cunningham), Walters (Cunningham sedan), Allard (Allard-Chrysler), and Johnson (Nash-Healey). And at Tertre Rouge, where the cars stream out to the Mulsanne Straight, Walters led the race with his Kamm-bodied Cunningham closed coupe, Fitch second, Moss third. And as they completed the lap it was Walters, then Moss, Simon (4.1 Ferrari).

Ill fortune struck some people early. Poore, who had been ill until the eve of the race, lost important gears on his Aston Martin. Ascari had clutch slip and was at his pit; Moran (2.6 Ferrari) was also in. Scaron on the ultra-light Simca retired. Stewart (Jaguar) stopped to report cooling trouble. Parnell (Aston Martin coupe) went out after a few laps with back axle trouble.

Ascari took the lead for two laps and then had his trouble, whereupon Simon took the lead from the Cunningham. The Mercedes-Benz in line ahead lay well placed, running about sixth, seventh, and eighth.

The Jaguars ran smack into radiator trouble, due probably to the new super-streamlined body and altered header tank, and one by one the three cars retired. One works Aston was left after the first three hours (Macklin-Collins).

On the second lap Chinetti (4.1 Ferrari) lapped at 105.63, fractionally higher than Moss's record last year. Ascari circulated at 106.08 mph and then had more clutch trouble. Carter took over the Cunningham and soon spent an hour and a half digging his car out of the sand at Mulsanne.

At about the same time Simon ran into worries, and now Manzon, in the astonishingly fast 2.3 Gordini, shot into the lead. With the disappearance of so many cars, the order became:

Manzon-Behra *(Gordini)*
Kling-Klenk *(Mercedes-Benz)*
Fitch-Rice *(Cunningham)*
Rosier-Trintignant *(Ferrari)*
Helfrich-Niedermayer *(Mercedes-Benz)*
Levegh *(Talbot)*

Between 9 and 10 P.M. the Ferrari attack faded as Simon fell right back, and the confident "Mercs" were shaken when Kling lost about 30 minutes at his pit with a dynamo defect. Did his team remember 1930, when Caracciola was put out with the same trouble? However, he got going, but was off the leader board now, so that at quarter distance the amazing Gordini had averaged 102.1 mph, the Talbot (Levegh still driving without relief) 101 mph, and the Mercedes just on 100 mph!

During the eighth hour the de-ditched Cunningham and Gatsonide's Jowett Jupiter made their exits and the Allard was taken by the DB3; but, this apart, the forty cars remaining kept their places during the fine, clear night until Saturday went into Sunday.

The bright promise of the Cunninghams was now tarnished, with two cars out and the remaining "ewe lamb" of the owner and Bill Spear placed only twelfth, just ahead of a Lancia Aurelia.

Just before 1:30 A.M. the fantastic Gordini refueled without losing the lead, and the problem for this pit and for that of the Levegh Talbot was quite simple—just to keep on keeping on. Neubauer's headache was whether he should rely on the French cars cracking or, alternatively, start to cut down arrears which had mounted up to about 12 minutes in 110 laps, or, say, 7 seconds per lap. And which of his drivers should take up the chase—the faster "new boys" or the experienced Lang?

Kling, with a damaged dynamo, was already regarded as a doubtful finisher, and duly retired at 1:45 A.M., just as Levegh's Talbot refueled. Still Levegh would not yield the driving seat to his co-driver. Was he attempting the whole run solo? It hardly seemed possible. He went off at a very hearty crack to receive a neon-light signal that he was lapping at 101.3 mph. So at 2 A.M.—ten hours gone—the line-up was almost unchanged from 10 P.M.

Mist turned to fog and speeds fell every lap; but there were no sensations, and the leaders held their places as though they were 100-mph trolley cars. The order of the nations at the eleventh hour was France, Germany, Italy, England, and U.S.A., and the first half of the race had been a disappointment to the large number of British enthusiasts who had flocked to France this year.

Drama: Manzon driving the Gordini came into the pits just after 3 A.M. as a glorious dawn began to tint the eastern sky, heralding a day of great heat. They worked on the engine and on the brakes. But whatever was wrong

*Two of the Mercedes team entering the first bend of
the notorious Le Mans Esses.*

under the hood, the brake trouble was decisive, and Levegh's Talbot roared into the lead, followed three laps
away by the Macklin-Collins Aston Martin, still running
to rule and going well in fifth place. They disqualified
Chinetti (Ferrari)—three times a winner at Le Mans—for
a mistake in refueling one lap too soon. Allard's Allard was
in trouble, having worked up with a gallant drive into fifth
place, and Nigel Mann's Aston broke the dynamo bracket
and lost all its amps.

By 8 A.M. when the weary pit personnel had shaved

and got their second wind and the drivers got down to the start of the "real race," the order was:

> Levegh (*Talbot*) 189 laps completed
> Helfrich-Niedermayer (*Mercedes-Benz*)
> Lang-Reiss (*Mercedes-Benz*)
> Macklin-Collins (*Aston Martin*)

As the morning wore on—rarely do hours pass so quickly—the race stabilized. Levegh was out in front, always with his three laps lead, although he was getting very tired, having driven the whole way, and was apt to hit grass verges and scrape sandbanks. Behind raced the two Mercedes (but Helfrich hit something and bent a wheel), the Macklin-Collins Aston ran fourth, and now, after a determined drive, in fifth place came Johnson and Wisdom in the Nash-Healey.

At half-past eleven the Aston stopped with a smoking-hot back end, which took two guns of oil, and was off again, and a few minutes later Johnson took over from Wisdom on the Nash-Healey after refueling, still firmly fifth, one lap behind the Aston. The Mercedes had given up trying to catch Levegh. They lost most of their three laps during the night fog which cost Levegh some ten seconds a lap against the Germans' forty. Macklin passed, making signs of resignation, and the Becquart-Wilkins Jupiter, sole survivor of the 1,500-cc. class (where the Porsches had seemed so threatening) went around touring to finish. Martial nearly killed himself pushing his OSCA coupe for several miles to his pit in the heat, but the repairs were impossible. First on Index of Performance at this stage was

144

The winning Mercedes-Benz winding through the Esses
on the way to victory.
MERCEDES-BENZ PHOTO

Hemard's 612-cc. Panhard, with Helfrich's Mercedes second and Lang's third, Levegh fourth.

Very gradually Levegh eased up at noon, lapping at about 98.5 mph with four laps (nearly 35 miles) in hand; Lang passed the obviously slowing Helfrich into second place; Macklin and Collins in the Aston raced steadily at about 91 mph third; the Nash-Healey fourth; and Chaboud (Talbot) was plugging away after it only 21 minutes behind and gaining—in fact he was the only driver among the leaders who was trying hard to catch anyone at all. Then came another bitter blow. At 1 P.M., after twenty-one hours of this terrific race, the last DB3 Aston vanished on the far side of the course, leaving the private entry of Clark-Keen in the DB2 radio-controlled car to carry the Aston flag, which they were doing with resolution. Levegh still circulated at just over 98 mph with ease and five laps in hand at 1 P.M. (three hours to go), but he was becoming very tired indeed. At 2 P.M. he slowed to 97.4 mph, which meant that Lang's Mercedes was going a little faster but still four and half laps behind, and the Nash-Healey, firmly fourth, was lapping at 94.6 mph. Then Chaboud ran off the road and the steady Cunningham, which had been driven most of the way by Briggs Cunningham (but was taken over by a stratagem by Bill Spear at 1 P.M.) came up into fifth place, eleven laps behind the British car—both running with American engines, incidentally.

So the clock ticked off the minutes toward the last hour of this tremendous race, run at record speed. And then came the final drama. With an hour and a quarter to go, Levegh came down to White House corner and heard a ghastly rattle which meant a broken connecting rod, and his race was run with four laps in hand! Automatically the Mercedes-Benz led and the field moved up one notch. France and Talbot had been robbed of a magnificent victory.

THE MOTOR, *June 18, 1952*

This report was completed within a few hours of the finish of the race in order to meet a copy deadline. It was not known until later that the connecting rod of Levegh's Talbot had broken through a sudden strain thrust upon it, almost certainly as a result of the driver engaging a lower gear than he intended when accelerating away from Arnage. A driver of his experience could not have committed such an error if he had not been in the last extremes of weariness. This is how one journalist, Georges Fraichard, described Pierre Levegh shortly before his car broke down. "When he came in to refuel for the last time, about three hours before the end of the race, I went down to have a look at him. Before me I saw an absolutely exhausted man, completely worn out, who could hardly remain on his feet. His eyes were staring. He did not recognize me. I expected him to ask René Marchand, a steady young man some thirty years of age, to take over, or at least that his followers would insist on him resting for a few minutes. Marchand could, without loss of prestige, have driven very cautiously (the lead which Levegh had built up permitted this) until on the penultimate lap Levegh could have resumed and, as he hoped, cross the line a winner.

"But no! Obstinate, and showing the terrible strain, Pierre Levegh climbed back into the car to the cheers of the ignorant spectators." Shortly afterward the loudspeakers announced that the Talbot had stopped between

Levegh in the last stages of weariness
before disaster struck.
KLEMANTASKI PHOTO

Arnage and White House. A few minutes later the official car, according to Fraichard, "brought back to his pit an almost lifeless dummy, who collapsed, vomiting, in a dark corner where two hours earlier a headstrong Levegh would have been wise to rest."

And the moral? I suppose that it takes a good deal more than courage to win a long-distance motor race! Three years later in this same event at Le Mans poor Levegh crashed into the crowd in his 300SLR Mercedes-Benz, killing himself and nearly a hundred of his fellow countrymen in the crowd.

148

LE MANS 1952 RESULTS		
1ST	H. Lang F. Reiss	Mercedes-Benz 96.67 mph average
2ND	G. Helfrich H. Niedermayer	Mercedes-Benz
3RD	L. Johnson T. Wisdom	Nash-Healey

CHAPTER NINE:

Every year from 1927 to 1957, with a brief break for World War II, as many as six hundred Italians who enjoy driving fast on their own roads took their cars along to the northern city of Brescia to take part in the biggest, most fascinating, and most dangerous sports car race on the calendar. More cars were entered as teams by the leading manufacturers. This was the Mille Miglia, or Thousand Miles, race for all classes of cars from staid-looking sedans and bubble cars to out-and-out racing sports cars

FASTEST AROUND ITALY

that were little different from Grand Prix racers. If the event did not cover the entire Italian peninsula, the roads over which the Mille Miglia was run covered the whole of that country's northern plain, twice crossed the Apennine mountain chain, and ran up the west coast from Rome to Florence. During the last weeks preceding this annual event many of the people of Italy were seized with the same sort of excitement and passionate interest in the race that is experienced in America before a World Series. Conver-

sation everywhere tended to concentrate passionately on the fancied cars. The more famous drivers gathered enthusiastic fans about them wherever they went and were cheered as they passed during practice. Mille Miglia week became something of a national festival.

As the speed of the fastest cars rose from 45 to 60

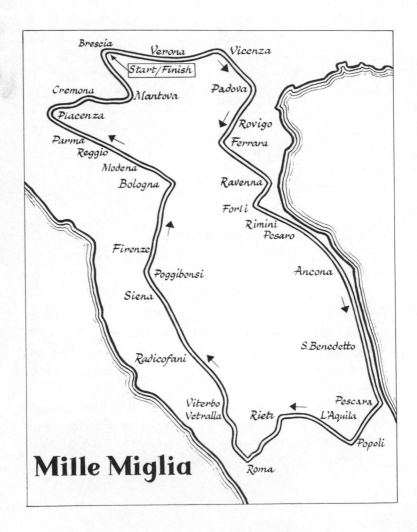

Mille Miglia

mph and then to more than 80 mph, the accident rate rose heavily. In the last years it was not unusual for twenty or thirty spectators and drivers to be killed or injured. That the figures were not higher was due to the extraordinary skill with which Italians always drive, whether or not they are racing; and they race most of the time anyway, even when they are not taking part in the Mille Miglia! For the Mille Miglia was run along ordinary roads, up and down mountain passes, through towns and villages with narrow streets and tramlines, over numerous level crossings, and straight through the heart of Italy's capital, Rome, and several other great cities. The Mille Miglia was finally stopped by the Italian government after the 1957 race, in which the casualty rate was particularly high and many spectators were tragically killed.

In 1955 the fastest Mille Miglia of all time was won by a British driver in a German car. During most of its life this race had been an Italian preserve. Few people came to challenge the Italian cars and drivers, and when they did they were nearly always defeated. The Italians have always built some of the fastest sports cars in the world, and in the Mille Miglia their drivers had the great advantage of running on home ground, where they knew the roads so much better than foreign drivers. Until 1955 Italian cars had won every year since World War II. But in that year the German firm of Mercedes-Benz decided to introduce their new racing sports car, the eight-cylinder fuel-injection 3-liter 300SLR model. This was almost exactly the same car as their all-conquering Grand Prix machine, but of course with two seats. It was tremendously fast, but so were the Italian Ferraris and Maseratis. The Mercedes-Benz competitions department decided to take

153

on the Italians. They had tried once before, in 1952, and had nearly succeeded.

When this German firm goes motor racing, it is always tremendously thorough about it. The cars are very carefully prepared. They make sure they engage the best drivers of the day. For the 1955 season they had the two fastest drivers in the world, Juan Manuel Fangio of the Argentine and Stirling Moss of Britain. Stirling Moss, too, has always believed in the most thorough preparations for any race. He decided that although he could not hope to learn every bend and corner, rise and fall, in the 1,000 miles of road along which he would be racing, he might make up for this handicap by taking along with him as passenger an observer who, with written notes painstakingly compiled over the previous weeks, could warn him by hand signals of the degree of severity of the corners and gradients. The man he took with him was Denis Jenkinson, the Continental correspondent of the magazine Motor Sport *and a man steeped in the traditions and skills of all forms of motor racing. The following story is his account of the race as seen from the passenger compartment of the Mercedes. It is in my opinion the most graphic and exciting record of a motor race ever written.*

I should first explain that in the Mille Miglia the cars were started one at a time and at one minute intervals from a wooden ramp built in the center of the main square in Brescia, each one sent on its way amid cheers from the crowds packed densely on all sides, leaving only the narrowest path for the cars' departure. During the hours of darkness—it took more than eight hours to get all the cars away—the scene was a wonderful and spectacular one. The numbers on the cars corresponded with their starting time.

154

*In the 1955 race Stirling Moss's number was 722; he there-
fore left at twenty-two minutes past seven. To insure that
all the cars followed the correct route and did not take
short cuts, and also to keep some sort of order in the race,
every car had to carry a card and a disk on the steering
column, which had to be stamped by officials at certain control points along the thousand-mile route.*

    *Stirling Moss's deadliest rivals in the race were the
Italian drivers Maglioli, Taruffi, Castellotti, and Marzotto, all of them driving Ferraris with more powerful engines than that of his Mercedes-Benz.*

THE CHIEF CONTESTANTS	
DRIVERS	CARS
Stirling Moss (Britain)	Mercedes-Benz 300SLR 3 liters (Germany)
J. M. Fangio (Argentina)	Mercedes-Benz 300SLR 3 liters (Germany)
H. Kling (Germany)	Mercedes-Benz 300SLR 3 liters (Germany)
H. Herrmann (Germany)	Mercedes-Benz 300SLR 3 liters (Germany)
E. Castellotti (Italy)	Ferrari 4.4 liters (Italy)
P. Taruffi (Italy)	Ferrari 3.7 liters (Italy)
U. Maglioli (Italy)	Ferrari 3.7 liters (Italy)
P. Marzotto (Italy)	Ferrari 3.7 liters (Italy)
G. Perdisa (Italy)	Maserati 3 liters (Italy)

BY DENIS JENKINSON

My enthusiasm for the Mille Miglia race goes back many years, among the reasons being the fact that it is permissible to carry a passenger. I had been a passenger in 1954, and after this experience I soon set about making plans for the 1955 event.

In September, while in discussion with the American driver John Fitch, we came to the decision that the only way a non-Italian could win the Mille Miglia was by applying science. At the time Fitch was hoping to be in the official Mercedes-Benz team for the event, and we had long talks about ways in which the driver could use a passenger as a mechanical brain, to remove the responsibility of learning the circuit. When it is realized that the race is over 1,000 miles (thus the name Mille Miglia) of ordinary, unprepared Italian roads, the only concession to racing being that all traffic is removed from the roads for the duration of the race, and the way through towns is lined with straw bales, it will be appreciated that the task of one man learning every corner, every swerve, gradient, hummock, brow, and railway crossing is nigh impossible. Even the top Italian drivers, such as Taruffi, Maglioli, Castellotti, etc., only know sections of the route perfectly, and all the time they must concentrate on remembering what lies around the next corner or over the next brow.

During the winter of 1954-1955 Moss joined the Mercedes-Benz team and the firm decided that it would not be possible for Fitch to drive for them in the Mille Miglia, though he would be in the team for Le Mans, so all our plans looked to be of no avail. Then just before Christmas a telephone call from Moss invited me to be his passenger in the Mille Miglia in a Mercedes-Benz 300SLR, an invitation which I promptly accepted, John Fitch having sportingly agreed that it would be a good thing for me to try out our plans for beating the Italians with Moss as driver.

When I met Moss early in the new year to discuss the event I already had some definite plan of action. Over lunch it transpired that he had very similar plans of using the passenger as a second brain to look after navigation. When we pooled our accumulated knowledge and ideas a great deal of groundwork was covered quickly. From four previous Mille Miglia races with Jaguars, Moss had gathered together a good quantity of notes about bumpy railway crossings, blind hill-brows, dangerous corners, and so on; and as I knew certain sections of the course intimately. All this knowledge put down on paper amounted to about 25 per cent of the circuit.

Early in February Mercedes-Benz were ready to start practicing, the first outing being in the nature of a test for the prototype 300SLR. While doing this testing I made copious notes, some of them rather like Chinese due to trying to write at 150 mph. When we stopped for lunch or for the night, we spent the whole time discussing the roads we had covered and transcribing my notes. The things we concentrated on were places where we might break the car, such as very bumpy railway crossings, sudden dips in the road, bad surfaces, tramlines, and so on. Then we logged all the difficult corners, grading them as "saucy," "dodgy," and "very dangerous," having a hand sign to indicate each type. Then we logged slippery surfaces, using another hand sign, and as we went along Moss indicated his interpretation of the conditions, while I pinpointed the place by a kilometer stone, plus or minus. Our task was eased greatly by the fact that there is a stone at every kilometer on Italian roads, and they are numbered in huge black figures, facing oncoming traffic.

In addition to all the points around the course where a mistake might mean an accident, and there are hundreds of them, we also logged all the long straights and everywhere that we could travel at maximum speed even though visibility was restricted, and again there were dozens of such points. Throughout all this preliminary work Moss impressed upon me at every possible moment the importance of not making any mistakes, such as indicating a brow to be flat-out when in reality it was followed by a tight left-hand bend. I told him he need not worry, for any accident he might have was going to involve me as well, as I was going to be by his side until the race was finished. After our first practice session we sorted out all our notes and had them typed out into some semblance of order, and before leaving England again I spent hours with a friend checking and cross-checking, going over the whole list many times, finally being 100 per cent certain that there were no mistakes.

On our second visit to Italy for more laps of the circuit we got down to fine details, grading some corners as less severe and others as much more so, especially as now we knew the way on paper, it meant that we arrived at many points much faster than previously when reconnoitering the route. On another lap I went the whole way, picking out really detailed landmarks that I would be able to see no matter what the conditions, whether we had the sun in our eyes or it was pouring with rain, and for this work we found Moss's Mercedes-Benz 220A saloon most useful, as it would cruise at an easy 85 mph and at the same time we could discuss any details.

Our whole plan was now nearing completion. We had seventeen pages of notes, and Moss had sufficient confidence in me to take blind brows at 90 to 100 mph, believing me when I said the road went straight on, though he freely admitted that he was not sure whether he would do the same thing at 170 mph in the race, no matter how confident I was. He said he'd probably ease back to 160, for though that 10 mph would make no difference to the resulting crash if I had made a mistake, it comforted him psychologically! Throughout all this training we carefully kept a log of our running time and average speeds, some of which were positively indecent and certainly not for publication, but the object was to find out which parts of the 1,000 miles dropped the overall average and where we could make up time. Our various averages in the 220A, the 300SL, and the 300SLR gave us an extremely interesting working knowledge of how the Mille Miglia might be won or lost.

Our second practice period ended in an accident and a smashed 300SL coupe, for Italian army trucks turn across your bow without warning just as English ones do. Rather crestfallen, we anticipated the rage of team-chief Neubauer when we reported this crash, but his only worry was whether we were personally damaged; the crashed car was of no importance; these things happened to everyone and anyway their only interest was to win the Mille Miglia, regardless of cost.

Leaving Italy for another brief respite, we both worried out every detail we could think about, from every aspect: the car, the route, our hand signals—for we could not converse in the 300SLR—any emergencies that might arise, anywhere we could save seconds, details of our own personal comfort which would avoid fatigue, and so on. We lived and breathed Mille Miglia day in and day out, leaving no idea untried. The joy of all this was that Daimler-Benz were doing exactly the same things on the mechanical side, supervised by engineers Uhlenhaut, Kosteletzky, and Werner, while the racing department was working unceasingly and Neubauer was worrying out every detail of the race organization in Italy. We were putting all our efforts into this race, knowing that they were negligible in comparison with those of the factory.

After Easter we went out to Brescia for our third and final practicing session, the technical department, with Kling and Herrmann, having already made an extra one. During their practice period they had thrashed the prototype car up and down the section from Rome to Florence, for this part of the route was the hardest. There are few straights, but all the time the car is averaging nearly 100 mph and the chassis is being subjected to strains from every possible angle; and as the 58-gallon gasoline tank would be full when leaving Rome, this part of the route would be the most likely one on which a breakdown would occur.

By now our details of the route were perfected and I now wrote them all down on a special sheet of paper eighteen feet in length. Moss had had an alloy case made, on the map-roller system, and for our final practice I employed this machine, winding the paper from the lower roller to the upper one, the notes being read through a

Perspex window, sealed with Sellotape in the event of the race being run in rain. A complete lap in a 300SL was done as a sort of dress rehearsal. This car was ideal as it had a maximum of nearly 140 mph, good acceleration, and was a very good approach to racing conditions, while at the same time we could speak to each other if the need arose, though normally all our conversation was done by hand signals, there being about fifteen altogether to cover every aspect of conversation. During this dress rehearsal we employed an amusing technique in the more deserted parts of the route, especially in the mountains, where I kept an eye on the approaching road out of the side windows and even out of the rear one on mountain hairpins. By my continually shouting "Yes" when the road was clear, Moss could have a real go at "nine-tenths" on the section of road just in front of him, certain in the knowledge that no traffic was approaching, for it must be remembered that all our practice was being done on normal Italian roads open to the public. This technique, while amusing to us, was also useful to Moss as it meant he could get the feel of the road surface conditions at racing speeds. By now the Mille Miglia date was approaching, and all around the 1,000 miles we saw more and more signs of growing enthusiasm, occasionally seeing other competitors practicing parts of the route, while the police were beginning to leap off the pavement, stop the traffic, and wave us on over crossroads with excited cries of *"Mille Miglia-via!"* Of course the Italian populace were leaping straight up into the air with joy as Moss fought the sliding SLR through many of the corners. It was interesting that the average English enthusiast would merely turn his head and look if he saw a 300SL being really motored, whereas the Italians, from errand boys to bank managers, will, at the same sight, spontaneously leave the ground and spin completely around, with excited waves, and then rush to another point in the hope of getting a further glimpse of the speeding car. We completed our third practice period without any crashes, though the "hack" SLR decided to give up the ghost while we were having a final run in it. But we were entirely blameless; old age creeps on the best vehicles, and this one had done the equivalent of at least six Mille Miglias in the hands of Moss, Fangio, Kling, and Herrmann, the four drivers for the race.

A week before the event we went to Stuttgart to try out the actual car we were using in the race, and several laps of the fast Hockenheim circuit convinced us that we had a truly magnificent 3-liter sports car under us, the eight-cylinder fuel-injection engine giving well over 290 bhp on normal pump gasoline, and the car geared to give a maximum of 170 mph at the peak revolutions of 7,500 rpm, though we were given no ultimate limit should the car wind itself over this downhill. On this SLR the seats were made to measure for us, being cut-and-shut just as a tailor would make a suit, while every detail in the cockpit received our personal attention, and anything was altered to our desire without question. When we finally left the racing department at 5 P.M. on Tuesday, April 26, we had the pleasant feeling that we had just left an organization that knew no limit to the trouble they would go to in order that we might start the Mille Miglia with everything on our side.

Next day we flew to Brescia, and when we went around to the garage in the evening the cars were already there, having been driven down in the fast racing trucks overnight. We were now satisfied with almost everything we could think about; we had practiced wheel changing over and over again in case we had tire trouble, and I would add that we impressed the Mercedes-Benz mechanics by changing a rear wheel in 1 min. 25 sec. from stopping the car to starting off again. We had practiced fitting the temporary aluminum aero-screens that went in front of the Perspex screen should it be broken by a stone—Mercedes-Benz engineers remembering how Hermann Lang was nearly suffocated at 170 mph at Donington Park in 1938 when his windshield was broken. We had tried changing plugs; we had studied the details of the pipes of the fuel injection, the gasoline pumps, various important parts of the wiring system, how the hood catches functioned; we were given spare ignition keys, shown where numerous small spares were stowed should we stop by the roadside with minor trouble; and by the end of the week we felt extremely confident that we could give of our best in this toughest of motor races, lasting for more than ten hours over every known road condition, over mountains and through cities, for 1,000 miles.

On the Friday before the race we did a final test on the nearby Autostrada, to try out some windshield modifications to improve the airflow along the cockpit sides. Also Moss tried out a new mechanism fitted to the gear change that would prevent his changing from second gear to fifth gear. The gear gate is exposed with first left forward, second center rear, third center forward, fourth right rear, and fifth right forward. Being used to four-speed boxes, Moss was occasionally going across the gate from second to fifth, and when he told the engineers about this the racing department set to and designed, drew, and made an entirely foolproof link mechanism that fitted on the top of the gate to prevent this. Moss mentioned this on Tuesday afternoon; on Friday morning the new parts arrived in Brescia and he was trying out the mechanism before lunch—at such speed does a true racing department work.

During the week before the race I had been going to bed extremely early and getting up extremely early, a complete reversal of my normal life, for to suddenly get up at 6 A.M. gives me a feeling of desolation until well past mid-morning. Moss had been employing similar tactics, so that when we went down to the start at 6:30 A.M. on the morning of May 1 we were both feeling ready for anything.

All the previous week a truly Italian sun had blazed out of the sky every day, and reports assured us that race day would be perfectly dry and hot, so we anticipated race speeds being very high. I had a list of the numbers of all our more serious rivals, as well as many of our friends in slower cars, and also the existing record times to every control point around the course so that we would have an idea of how we were doing. We had privately calculated on an average of 90 mph—2 mph over the record of Marzotto, providing the car went well and the roads were dry. Mercedes-Benz gave us no orders, leaving the running of the race entirely to each driver, but insisted that the car be brought back to Brescia if humanly possible. Moss and I had made a pact that we would keep the car going as long as was practicable, having decided in practice at which point we could have the engine blow up and still coast in to the finish, and how many kilometers we were prepared to push it to finish or to a control. At Ravenna, Pescara, Rome, Florence, and Bologna there were Mercedes-Benz

164

pits, complete with all spares, changes of tire should it start to rain, food, drink, and assistance of every sort, for in this race there are no complicated rules about work done on the car or outside assistance; it is a free-for-all event.

The enormous entry had started to leave Brescia the previous evening at 9 P.M. while we were sleeping peacefully, the cars leaving at one-minute intervals, and it was not until 6:55 A.M. on Sunday morning that the first of the over-2,000-cc. sports cars left. It was this group that held the greatest interest, for among the 34 entries lay the outright winner of this race, though many of the 2-liter Maseratis and smaller Oscas and Porsches could not be overlooked. Starting positions were arranged by ballot beforehand and the more important to us were Fangio 658, Kling 701, Collins (Aston Martin) 702, Herrmann 704, Maglioli (Ferrari) 705; then there went off a group of slower cars, and Carini (Ferrari) 714, Scotti (Ferrari) 718, Pinzero (Ferrari) 720, and then us at 7:22 A.M. There was no hope of seeing our teammates, for they left too long before us, as did Maglioli, but we were hoping to catch Carini before the end. Our big worry was not so much those in front as those behind, for there followed Castellotti (Ferrari 4.4 liter) 723, Sighinolfi (Ferrari 3.7 liter) 724, Paulo Marzotto (Ferrari 3.7 liter) 727, and, finally, the most dangerous rival of them all, that master tactician, Taruffi (Ferrari 3.7 liter) 728. With all these works Ferraris behind us we could not hang about in the opening stages, for Castellotti was liable to catch us, and Sighinolfi would probably scrabble past us, using the grass banks, he being that sort of driver, and Marzotto would stop at nothing to beat the German cars. So if we didn't press on straight away there was a good chance of the dice becoming a little exciting, not to say dangerous, in the opening 200 miles.

Neubauer was ever present at the start, warning Moss to give the car plenty of throttle as he left the starting ramp, for Herrmann had nearly fluffed his take-off. He also assured us that we could take the dip at the bottom of the ramp without worrying about grounding. The mechanics had warmed the engine and they pushed the car up onto the starting platform to avoid unnecessary strain on the single-plate clutch, one of the weak points of the 300SLR. The route card which we had to get stamped at the various controls round the course was securely attached to a board and already fitted in its special holder, the board being attached by a cord to one of my grab rails, to avoid losing it in the excitement of any emergency. We both settled down in our seats, Moss put his goggles on, I showed him a note at the top of my roller device, warning him not to apply the brakes fiercely on the first corner, for the bi-metal drums needed a gentle application to warm them after standing for two days.

Thirty seconds before 7:22 A.M. he started the engine, the side exhaust pipes blowing a cloud of smoke over the starter and Sig. Castegnato and Count Maggi, the two men behind this great event, and then as the flag fell we were off with a surge of acceleration and up to peak revs in first, second, and third gears, weaving our way through the vast crowds lining the sides of the road. Had we not been along this same road three times already in an SLR amid the hurly-burly of morning traffic, I should have been thoroughly frightened; but now with the roads ahead of us clear, I thought, Moss could really get down to some uninterrupted motoring. We had the sun shining full in our

166

eyes, which made navigation difficult, but I had written the notes over and over again, and gone over the route in my imagination so many times that I almost knew it by heart. One of the first signals was to take a gentle S-bend through a village on full throttle in fourth gear, and as Moss did this, being quite unable to see the road for more than 100 yards ahead, I settled down to the job, confident that our scientific methods of equaling the Italians' ability at open-road racing was going to work. At no time before the race did we ever contemplate getting into the lead, for we fully expected Fangio to set the pace, with Kling determined to win at all costs, so we were out for a third place and to beat all the Ferraris. Barely 10 miles after the start we saw a red speck in front of us and had soon nipped by on a left-hand curve. It was 720, Pinzero, number 721 being a non-starter. By my right hand was a small grab rail and a horn button; the steering was on the left of the cockpit, by the way, and this button not only blew the horn, but also flashed the lights, so that while I played a fanfare on this Moss placed the car for overtaking other competitors. My direction indications I was giving with my left hand, so what with turning the map roller and feeding Moss with sucking sweets there was never a dull moment. The car was really going well now, and on the straights to Verona we were getting 7,500 in top gear, a speed of 274 kph, or as close to 170 mph as one could wish to travel. On some of these long straights our navigation system was paying handsomely, for we could keep at 170 mph over blind brows, even when overtaking slower cars, Moss sure in the knowledge that all he had to do was to concentrate on keeping the car on the road and traveling as fast as possible. This in itself was more than enough, but he was

167

sitting back in his usual relaxed position, making no apparent effort until some corners were reached when the speed at which he controlled slides, winding the wheel from right to left and back again, showed that his superb reflexes and judgment were on top of their form.

Cruising at maximum speed, we seemed to spend most of the time between Verona and Vicenza passing Austin-Healeys that could not have been doing much more than 115 mph. With flashing light, horn blowing, and a wave of the hand we went by as though we were touring. Approaching Padova, Moss pointed behind and I looked around to see a Ferrari gaining on us rapidly, and with a grimace of disgust at one another we realized it was Castellotti. The Mercedes-Benz was giving all it had, and Moss was driving hard but taking no risks, letting the car slide just so far on the corners and no more. Entering the main street of Padova at 150 mph, we braked for the right-angled bend at the end, and suddenly I realized that Moss was beginning to work furiously on the steering wheel, for we were arriving at the corner much too fast and it seemed doubtful whether we could stop in time. I sat fascinated, watching Moss working away to keep control, and I was so intrigued to follow his every action and live every inch of the way with him that I completely forgot to be scared. With the wheels almost on locking point he kept the car straight to the last possible fraction of a second, making no attempt to get around the corner, for that would have meant a complete spin and then anything could happen. Just when it seemed we must go head-on into the straw bales Moss got the speed low enough to risk letting go the brakes and try taking the corner, and as the front of the car slid over the dry road we went bump! into the bales with our left-hand front corner, bounced off into the middle of the road and, as the car was then pointing in the right direction, Moss selected bottom gear and opened out again.

All this time Castellotti was right behind us, and as we bounced off the bales he nipped by us, grinning over his shoulder. As we set off after him, I gave Moss a little hand-clap of appreciation for showing me just how a really great driver acts in a difficult situation.

Through Padova we followed the 4.4-liter Ferrari and on acceleration we could not hold it, but the Italian was driving like a maniac, sliding all the corners, using the pavements and the loose edges of the road. Around a particularly dodgy left-hand bend on the outskirts of the town I warned Moss and then watched Castellotti sorting out his Ferrari, the front wheels on full under-steer, with the inside one off the ground, and rubber pouring off the rear tires, leaving great wide marks on the road. This was indeed motor racing from the best possible position, and beside me was a quiet, calm young man who was following the Ferrari at a discreet distance, ready for any emergency. Out of the town we joined an incredibly fast stretch of road, straight for many miles, and we started alongside the Ferrari in bottom gear, but try as the Mercedes-Benz did the red car just drew away from us, and once more Moss and I exchanged very puzzled looks. By the time we had reached our maximum speed the Ferrari was over 200 yards ahead, but then it remained there, the gap being unaltered along the whole length of the straight. At the cut-off point at the end we gained considerably, both from the fact that we knew exactly when the following left-hand corner was approaching and also from slightly superior brakes. More full-throttle running saw us keeping the

Ferrari in sight, and then as we approached a small town we saw Castellotti nip past another Ferrari, and we realized we were going to have to follow through the streets until there was room to pass. It was number 714, Carini, so soon, and this encouraged Moss to run right around the outside of the Ferrari, on a right-hand curve, confident from my signals that the road would not suddenly turn left. This very brief delay had let Castellotti get away from us but he was not completely out of sight, and after waving to Peter Collins, who had broken down by the roadside before Rovigo, we went into that town at terrific speed. Straight across the square we went, where in practice we had had to go around the island; broadside we left the last right turn of the town, with the front wheels on full opposite lock and the throttle pedal hard down. Castellotti was in sight once more, but out on the open roads he was driving so near the limit that on every corner he was using the gravel and rough stuff on the edges of the road. This sent up huge a huge cloud of dust, and we could never be sure whether or not we were going to enter it to find the Ferrari sideways across the road or bouncing off the banks and trees, for this sort of hazard a scientific route-navigating method could not cope with. Wisely Moss eased back a little and the Ferrari got ahead of us sufficiently to let the dust clouds settle.

Along the new road by the side of the River Po we overtook Lance Macklin in his Austin-Healey, and he gave us a cheery wave, and then we went through Ferrara, under the railway bridge, over the traffic lights and down the main streets and out onto the road to Ravenna. All the way along there were signs of people having the most almighty incidents, black marks from locked wheels making the weirdest patterns on the road, and many times on corners we had signaled as dangerous or dodgy we came across cars in the touring categories lying battered and bent by the roadside, sure indication that our grading of the corner was not far wrong. To Ravenna the road winds a great deal and now I could admire the Moss artistry as he put in some very steady "nine-tenths" motoring, especially on open bends around which he could see and on those that he knew. The way he would control the car with throttle and steering wheel long after all four tires had reached the breakaway point was a sheer joy, and most difficult to do justice to with mere pen and paper. Approaching the Ravenna control I took the route-card board from its holder and held it up for Moss to see, to indicate that we had to stop here to receive the official stamp. As we braked toward the CONTROLLO banner across the road and the black-and-white checkered line on the road itself, amid waving flags and numerous officials, I held my right arm well out of the car to indicate to them which side we wanted the official with the rubber stamp to be. With me holding the board on the side of the cockpit we crossed the control line. Bang! went the rubber stamp, and we were off without actually coming to rest. Just beyond the control were a row of pits and there was 723, Castellotti's Ferrari, having some tire changes, which was not surprising in view of the way he had been driving.

With a scream of "Castellotti!" Moss accelerated hard around the next corner and we twisted our way through the streets of Ravenna, nearly collecting an archway in the process, and then out on the fast winding road to Forli. Our time to Ravenna had been well above the old record, but Castellotti had got there before us and we had

171

no idea how Taruffi and the others behind us were doing. Now Moss continued the pace with renewed vigor and we went through Forli, waving to the garage that salvaged the SL we crashed in practice, down the fast winding road to Rimini, with another wave to the Alfa Romeo service station that looked after the SLR that broke its engine. I couldn't help thinking that we had certainly left our mark around the course during practice. Ever since leaving the start we had had the rising sun shining in our eyes, and now with the continual effects of sideways "G" on my body, my poor stomach was beginning to suffer and, together with the heat from the gearbox by my left buttock, the engine fumes, and the nauseating brake-lining smells from the inboard-mounted brakes, it cried "enough" and what little breakfast I had eaten went overboard, together with my spectacles, for I made the fatal mistake of turning my head sideways at 150 mph with my goggles lowered. Fortunately I had a spare pair, and there was no time to worry about a protesting stomach, for we were approaching Pesaro, where there was a sharp right corner.

Now the calm, blue Adriatic Sea appeared on our left and we were on the long coastal straights, taking blind brows and equally blind bridges at our full 170 mph, and I chuckled to myself as I realized that Moss was not lifting his foot as he had threatened. We were beginning to pass earlier numbers very frequently now, among them some 2-liter Maseratis being driven terribly slowly, a couple of TR2 Triumphs running in convoy, and various saloons, with still numerous signs of the telling pace: a wrecked Giulietta on the right, a 1,100-cc. Fiat on the left, a Ferrari coupe almost battered beyond recognition, and a Renault that had been rolled up into a ball. Through An-

172

*Moss and Jenkinson flash through Ancona at 150 mph
in their Mercedes-Benz.*

KLEMANTASKI PHOTO

cona the crowds were beautifully controlled, barriers keeping them back on the pavements, and we were able to use
the full width of the road everywhere; and up the steep
hill leaving the town we stormed past more touring-car
competitors who had left in the small hours of the morning
while we were still asleep. All this time there had been no
sign of any of our close rivals. We had passed the last of
the Austin-Healeys, driven by Abecassis, a long way back,
and no Ferrari had appeared in our rear-view mirror.

It was a long way down to the next control point at
Pescara, and we settled down to cruising at our maximum
speed, the car giving no impression at all of how fast it was
traveling until we overtook another competitor—who, I
knew, must be doing 110 mph—or when I looked sideways
at the trees and hedges flashing past. It was now mid-morn-

173

ing and the sun was well above us but still shining down
into our faces and making the cockpit exceedingly hot, in
spite of having all the air vents fully open. Through the
dusty, dirty Adriatic villages we went, and all the time I
gave Moss the invaluable hand signals that were taking
from him the mental strain of trying to remember the
route, though he still will not admit to how much mental strain he suffered convincing himself that I was not
making any mistakes in my 170 mph navigation. On one
straight lined with trees we had marked down a hump in
the road as being "flat-out" only if the road was dry. It
was, so I gave the appropriate signal, and in fifth gear
with 7,500 rpm on the tachometer we took off, for we had
made an error in our estimation of the severity of the
hump. For a measurable amount of time the vibro-massage
that you get sitting in a 300SLR at that speed suddenly
ceased, and there was time for us to look at each other with
raised eyebrows before we landed again. Even had we been
in the air for only one second we should have traveled some
200 feet through the air, and I estimated the duration of
flight at something more than one second. The road was
dead straight and the Mercedes-Benz made a perfect four-
point landing. I thankfully praised the driver that he
hadn't moved the steering wheel a fraction of an inch, for
that would have been our end. With the heat of the sun
and the long straights we had been getting into a complac-
ent stupor, but this little "moment" brought us back to
reality and we were fully on the job when we approached
Pescara. Over the railway crossing we went, far faster than
we had ever done in practice, and the car skated right
across the road, with all four wheels sliding, and I was sure
we were going to write off some gasoline pumps by the

roadside, but somehow the boy got control again and we merely brushed some straw bales and then braked heavily to a stop for the second control stamp. Approaching this point, I not only held the route card for the driver to see, but also pointed to the fuel filler, for here we were due to make our first refueling. However, I was too late. Moss was already pointing backward at the tank himself to tell me the same thing. Just beyond the control line we saw engineer Werner holding a blue flag bearing the Mercedes-Benz star, and as we stopped everything happened at once. Some 18 gallons of fuel went in from a gravity tank, just sufficient to get us to our main stop at Rome; the windshield was cleaned, for it was thick with dead flies; a hand gave me a slice of orange and a peeled banana, while another was holding a small sheet of paper; someone else was looking at the tires and Moss still had the engine running. On the paper was written "Taruffi, Moss 15 seconds, Herrmann, Kling, Fangio" and their times. I had just yelled, "Second, 15 seconds behind Taruffi!" when I saw a hand trying to switch off the ignition. I recognized the arm of an interfering policeman who seemed to think there was a danger of fire. I gave it a thump, and as I did so, Moss crunched in bottom gear and we accelerated away as hard as we could go. What had seemed like an age was actually only 28 seconds!

Over the bridge we went, sharp right, and then up one of the side turnings of Pescara toward the station where we were to turn right again. There was a blue Gordini just going round the corner and then I saw that we were overshooting, and with locked wheels we slid straight on, bang into the straw bales. I just had time to hope there was nothing solid behind the wall of bales, when the air was full of flying straw and we were on the pavement, Moss quickly selected bottom gear and without stopping he drove along the pavement behind the bales until he could bounce down off the curb and continue on his way, passing the Gordini in the process. As we went up through the gears on the long straight out of Pescara I kept an eye on the water temperature gauge, for that clonk certainly creased the front of the car and may have damaged the radiator or filled the intake with straw, but all seemed well; the temperature was still remaining constant. There followed three completely blind brows in quick succession and we took these at full speed, the effect being rather like a switchback at a fair, and then we wound and twisted our way along the barren valley between the rocky mountain sides to Popoli, where a Bailey bridge still serves to cross a river. Along this valley I saw the strange sight of about fifty robed monks, with shining bald pates, standing on a high mound and waving to us as we went by with a noise sufficient to wake the devil himself. Up into the mountains we climbed, sliding around the hairpins with that beautiful Moss technique. And then along the peculiar deserted plateau high up in the mountains we held our maximum speed for many kilometers, to be followed by a winding twisting road into Aquila, where up the main street the control was dealt with while still on the move. We certainly were not wasting any seconds anywhere and Moss was driving absolutely magnificently, right on the limit of adhesion all the time and more often than not over the limit, driving in that awe-inspiring narrow margin that you enter just before you have a crash if you have not the Moss skill, or those few yards of momentary terror you have on ice just before you go in the ditch. This masterly handling was no fluke;

he was doing it deliberately, his extra special senses and reflexes allowing him to go that much closer to the absolute limit than the average racing driver and way beyond the possibilities of normal mortals like you and me.

On the way to Rome we hit a railway crossing that had been just "bumpy" in the SL and smooth in the 220A; the resultant thud threw us high out of our seats into the airstream, and with a crash we landed back again, nearly breaking our spines, but the Mercedes-Benz suspension absorbed it all without protest and there was no feeling that anything had bottomed unduly severely. This sort of thing had happened three or four times already, for our route-noting was not infallible, and it seemed unbelievable that nothing broke on the car each time. Although we occasionally saw a train streaming along in the distance, we never came across any closed railway crossings, though if we had, we had a remedy. In practice we had tried lifting the barrier, Italian gates being two long poles that lower across the road, and found that the slack on the operating cables was just sufficient to allow the car to be driven under the pole, much to the annoyance of the crossing keeper. However, this did not arise and down into the Rome control we had a pretty clear run, being highly delighted to overtake Maglioli soon after Rieti, he suffering from an arm injury received in practice and a car that was not going well. With a grin at each other we realized that one of our unseen rivals was now disposed of, but we still had Taruffi behind us on the road, and no doubt well ahead of us on time, for all this ground was local color to him. Coming down off the mountain, we had overtaken Musso driving a 2-liter Maserati, and as we had calculated that we were unlikely ever to catch him even if we averaged 90 mph for the whole race, we realized we must be setting a fantastic record speed, but as Taruffi had been leading at Pescara, his average must be even higher.

The last six miles into the Rome control were an absolute nightmare. There were no corners that needed signals, and we would normally have done 150 to 160 mph, but the crowds of spectators were so thick that we just could not see the road, and the surface being bumpy, Moss dared not drive much over 130 mph because there was barely room for two cars abreast. It seemed that the whole of Rome was out to watch the race, and all oblivious of the danger of a high-speed racing car. While I blew the horn and flashed the lights Moss swerved the car from side to side and this had the effect of making those on the very edge leap hastily backward, thus giving us a little more room. The last mile into the control was better organized and I was able to show Moss the control card, point backward at the fuel tank and also at the fiber disk wired to the steering column, which had to be punched at this control. Bang! went the stamp and we then drew into the Mercedes-Benz pit and switched off the engine; this was our first real stop since leaving Brescia nearly 3½ hours ago, and our average speed to this point was 107 mph, the average to Pescara having been 118 mph, the mountain section causing it to drop from there to Rome.

As we stopped Moss leapt out to relieve himself. I felt the car rise up on the jacks and heard the rear hub nuts being beaten off, the windshield was cleaned, and a welcome shower of water sprinkled over me, for I was very hot, very tired, very dirty, oily, and sweaty and must have looked a horrible sight to spectators. The fuel tank was being filled, someone handed me a drink of mineral water and an orange, and offered a tray of sandwiches and cakes, but I felt incapable of eating anything firmer than a slice of orange. A hand appeared in front of me holding a sheet of paper and I snatched it and read "Moss, Taruffi, Herrmann, Kling, Fangio" and the times showed me had a lead of nearly two minutes. Bump! went the car as it was dropped down off the jacks, and with a lithe bound Moss was into the driving seat again. As we took the hairpin after the control I managed to yell in his ear, "First by more than one minute from Taruffi" and then the noise of the exhaust and wind prevented any further words. On the next bend we saw a silver Mercedes-Benz, number 701, well off the road among the trees and badly wrecked. We knew it was Kling and exchanged long faces with each other, wondering how badly hurt he was, but this had no effect on Moss and he now began to put everything he knew into his driving, on this most difficult section, while I had to concentrate hard in order to give him warnings and signals of the approaching road conditions, for this was indeed a difficult section for both of us. Past Monterosi we waved to the Agip service station, where we had had a sheep-killing incident in practice, and then we sped on our way through Bitterbo, sliding this way and that, leaving the ground on more occasions than I can remember, yet all the while feeling completely at ease, for such is the confidence that Moss gave me. Around the corners I never ceased to marvel at the superb judgment with which he weighed up the maximum possible speed at which he could go, and just how far he could let the car slide without going into the ditch or hitting a wall or rock face. Now there was the continual hazard of passing slower cars, though it must be recorded that most of them gave way splendidly, keeping one eye on the mirror. Just after Acquapendente I made my first and only mistake in navigating. That it was not serious is why you are reading these words now. Having just given warning of a very dodgy right-hand bend, I received a shower of petrol down my neck and looked around to see what had happened just as we arrived at another similar corner, and I missed the signal. Fortunately Moss had recognized the corner, for he knew many parts of the course extremely well. After seeing that the petrol was coming from the filler due to surge, I looked back to see an irate Moss face saying very rude things at me and shaking his fist, all the while cornering at a fantastic speed. How serious the fuel surge was I did not know. Since the exhaust pipes were on the side of the car, I decided it would be all right and said nothing to Moss, as he appeared not to have received any of the spray. For the next 10 or 15 miles I received this gentle spray of cold fuel, cooling in the enormous heat of the cockpit but a little worrying in case it got worse. Up the Radicofani Pass we stormed and the way the car leapt and slithered about would have really frightened me had I not already had a lot of experience of its capabilities and of the skill of Stirling Moss; as it was I sat there and reveled in the glorious feeling of really fast motoring. Over the top of the pass we swept past a saloon car competitor, into a downhill right-hand bend followed by a sharp left-hander. Previous to this Moss had been pointing to the front of the car and indicating that a brake was beginning to grab on occasions, and this was one of them. Without any warning the car spun and there was just time to think what a desolate part of Italy it was in which to crash, when I realized that we had almost stopped in our own length and were sliding gently into the ditch to land with a crunch that dented the tail. "This is all right," I thought; "we can probably push it out of this one," and I was about to start getting out when Moss selected bottom gear and we drove out—lucky indeed! Before we could point the car in the right direction we had to make two reverses, and as we accelerated away down the mountainside, I fiddled about putting the safety catch back on the reverse position of the gear gate, while we poked our tongues out at each other in mutual derision.

At the Siena control we had no idea of whether we were still leading or not, but Moss was quite certain that Taruffi would have had to have worked extremely hard to catch him, for he had put all he knew into that last part of the course, he told me afterward. Never relaxing for an instant, he continued to drive the most superb race of his career, twirling the steering wheel this way and that, controlling slides with a delicateness of throttle that was fairy-like, or alternately provoking slides with the full power of the engine in order to make the car change direction bodily. The now dirty, oily, and battered collection of machinery that had left Brescia gleaming like new still answered superbly to his every demand, the engine always being taken to 7,500 rpm in the gears, and on one occasion to 8,200 rpm—the excitement at that particular instant not allowing time for a gear change or an easing of the throttle; for the way Moss steered the car around the sharp corners with the back wheels was sheer joy to experience.

On the winding road from Siena to Florence physical strain began to tell on me, for with no steering wheel to give me a feel of what the car was going to do, my body was being continually subjected to terrific centrifugal forces as the car changed direction. The heat, fumes, and noise were becoming almost unbearable, but I gave myself renewed energy by looking at Stirling Moss who was sitting beside me completely relaxed, working away at the steering as if we had only just left Brescia instead of having been driving for nearly 700 miles under a blazing sun. Had I not known the route I would have happily got out there and then, having enjoyed every mile, but ahead lay some interesting roads over which we had practiced hard, and the anticipation of watching Moss really try over these stretches, with the roads closed to other traffic, made me forget all about the physical discomforts. I was reminded a little of the conditions when we approached one corner and some women got up and fled with looks of terror on their faces, for the battered Mercedes-Benz, dirty and oil-stained and making as much noise as a Grand Prix car, with two sweaty, dirty, oil-stained figures behind the windshield, must have looked terrifying to peaceful peasants as it entered the corner in a full four-wheel slide. The approaches of Florence were almost back-breaking as we bounced and leapt over the badly maintained roads and across the tramlines, and my heart went out to the driver of an orange Porsche who was hugging the crown of the steeply cambered road. He must have been shaken as we shot past with the left-hand wheels right down in the gutter. Down a steep hill in second gear we went, into third at peak revs, and I thought, "It's a brave man who can unleash nearly 300 bhp down a hill this steep and then change into a higher gear." At speeds between 120 and 130 mph we went through the streets of Florence, over the great river bridge, broadside across a square, across more tramlines, and into the control point. Now Moss had really got

182

the bit between his teeth; nothing was going to keep him from winning this race, I felt. He had a rather special look of concentration on his face and I knew that one of his greatest ambitions was to do the Florence-Bologna section in under one hour. This road crosses the heart of the Apennines by way of the Futa Pass and the Raticosa Pass, and though only just over 60 miles in length it is like a Prescott Hill-Climb all the way. As we got the route card stamped, again without coming to rest, I grabbed the sheet of paper from the Mercedes-Benz man at the control, but before I could read more than that we were still leading, it was torn from my grasp as we accelerated away among the officials. I indicated that we were still leading the race, and by the way Moss left Florence, as though at the start of a Grand Prix, I knew he was out to crack one hour to Bologna, especially as he also looked at his wristwatch as we left the control. "This is going to be fantastic," I thought as we screamed up the hills out of Florence. "He is really going to do some nine-tenths plus motoring." Between giving him direction signals I took a firm grip of the "struggling bar," keeping the left side of my body as far out of Moss's way as possible, for he was going to need all the room possible for his whirling arms and for stirring the gear lever about. Up into the mountains we screamed, occasionally passing other cars, such as 1,900 Alfa Romeos, 1,100 Fiats, and some small sports cars.

All the time I had found it very difficult to take my eyes off the road. I could have easily looked around me, for there was time, but somehow the whole while that Moss was really dicing I felt a hypnotic sensation forcing me to live every inch of the way with him. It was probably this factor that prevented me ever being frightened, for nothing arrived unexpectedly, I was keeping up with him mentally all the way, which I had to do if I wasn't to miss any of our route marking, though physically I had fallen away behind him and I marveled that anyone could drive so furiously for such a long time, for it was now well into the Sunday afternoon. At the top of the Futa Pass there were enormous crowds all waving excitedly, and on numerous occasions Moss nearly lost the car completely as we hit patches of melted tar, coated with oil and rubber from all the other competitors in front of us, and for nearly a mile he had to ease off and drive at a bare eight-tenths, the road was so tricky. Just over the top of the Futa we saw a Mercedes-Benz by the roadside amid a crowd of people; it was 704, young Hans Herrmann, and though we could not see him, we waved. The car looked undamaged so we assumed he was all right.

Now we simply had to get to Brescia first, I thought, we mustn't let Taruffi beat us. On we went, up and over the Raticosa Pass, plunging down the other side, in one long series of slides that to me felt completely uncontrolled but to Moss were obviously intentional. However, there was one particular one which was not intentional, and by sheer good fortune the stone parapet on the outside of the corner stepped back just in time, and caused us to make rude faces at each other. On a wall someone had painted VIVA PERDISA, VIVA MASERATI, and as we went past in a long controlled slide, we spontaneously both gave it the victory sign and had a quiet chuckle between ourselves in the cramped and confined space of our traveling hothouse and bath of filth and perspiration. On another part of the Raticosa amid great crowds of people we saw an enormous fat man in the road, leaping up and down with delight; it was the happy body-builder of the Maserati racing department, a good friend of Stirling's, and we waved back to him.

Down off the mountains we raced, into the broiling heat on the afternoon, into Bologna, along the dusty tramlined road, with hordes of spectators on both sides, but here beautifully controlled, so that we went into Bologna at close on 150 mph and down to the control point, Moss doing a superb bit of braking judgment even at this late stage in the race and in spite of brakes that were beginning to show signs of the terrific thrashing they had been receiving. Here we had the steering column disk punched again and the card stamped, and with another Grand Prix start we were away through the streets of Bologna so quickly that I didn't get the vital news sheet from our depot. Now we had no idea of where we lay in the race or what had happened to our rivals, but we knew we had crossed the mountains in 1 hr. 1 min. and were so far ahead of Marzotto's record that it seemed impossible. The hard part was now over, but Moss did not relax, for it had occurred to him that it was possible to get back to Brescia in the round 10 hours, which would make the race average 100 mph.

Up the long fast straights through Modena, Reggio Emilia, and Prama we went, not wasting a second anywhere, cruising at a continuous 170 mph, cutting off only where I indicated corners or bumpy hill brows. Looking up I suddenly realized that we were overtaking an airplane, and then I knew I was living in the realms of fantasy. It was flying at about 300 feet, filming our progress, and we must have looked most impressive from above, especially as we dropped back by going around the Fidenza by-pass only to catch up again on the main road.

This really was pure speed. The car was going perfectly and reaching 7,600 rpm in fifth gear in places, which was as honest a 170 mph plus as I'd care to argue about. Going into Piacenza where the road doubles back towards Mantova we passed a 2CV Citröen bowling along merrily, having left Brescia the night before, and then we saw a 2-liter Maserati which shook us perceptibly, for we thought we had passed them all long ago. It was number 621, Francesco Giardini, and appreciating just how fast he must have driven to reach this point before us, we gave him a salutary wave as we roared past, leaving Piacenza behind us. More important was the fact that we were leaving the sun behind us, for nice though it was to have dry roads to race on, the blazing sun had made visibility for both of us very tiring.

Through Cremona we went without relaxing, and now we were on the last leg of the course, there being a special prize and the Nuvolari Cup for the fastest speed from Cremona to Brescia. Although the road lay straight for most of the way, there were more than six villages to traverse as well as the final route-card stamp to get in the town of Mantova. In one village, less than 50 miles from the finish, we had an enormous slide on some melted tar. For a moment I thought we would hit a concrete wall, but with that absurdly calm manner of his, Moss tweaked the wheel this way and that and caught the car just in time, and with his foot hard down we went on our way as if nothing had happened. The final miles into Brescia were sheer joy, the engine singing round on full power, and after we had passed our final direction indication I put my roller map away and thought, "If it blows to pieces now, we can carry it the rest of the way." The last corner into the finishing area was taken in a long slide with the power and noise full on, and we crossed the finishing line at well over 100 mph, still not knowing that we had made motor-racing history, but happy and contented at having completed the whole race and done our best.

From the finishing line we drove around to the official garage, where the car had to be parked, and Stirling asked, "Do you think we've won?" to which I replied, "We must wait for Taruffi to arrive, and we don't know when Fangio got in." At the garage we were told that Taruffi was out, retired with a broken oil pump, and that Fangio was behind us. We had won. Yes, won the Mille Miglia, achieved the impossible, broken all the records, ruined all the Mille Miglia legends, made history. We clasped each other in delirious joy and would have wept, but we were too overcome and still found it hard to believe that we had won. Then we were swept away amid a horde of police and officials, and the ensuing crush amid the wildly enthusiastic crowds was harder to bear than the whole of the 1,000-mile grind we had just completed.

Our total time for the course was 10 hr. 7 min. 48 sec., an average of more than 157 kph (nearly 98 mph) and our average for the 85 miles from Cremona to Brescia had been 123 mph. As we were driven back to our hotel, tired, filthy, oily, and covered with dust and dirt, we grinned happily at each other's black face and Stirling said, "I'm so happy that we've proved that a Britisher can win the Mille Miglia, and that the legend 'He who leads at Rome never leads at Brescia' is untrue. Also I feel we have made up for the two cars we wrote off in practice." Then he gave a chuckle and said, "We've rather made a mess of the record, haven't we? Sort of spoiled it for anyone else, for there probably won't be another completely dry Mlle Miglia for twenty years."

It was with a justified feeling of elation that I lay in

a hot bath, for I had had the unique experience of being with Stirling Moss throughout his epic drive, sitting beside him while he worked as I have never seen anyone work before in my life, and harder and longer than I ever thought it possible for a human being to do. It was indeed a unique experience, the greatest experience in the whole of the twenty-two years I have been interested in motor racing, an experience that was beyond my wildest imagination, with a result that even now I find it extremely hard to believe.

After previous Mille Miglias I have said, "He who wins the Mille Miglia is some driver, and the car he uses is some sports car." I now say it again with the certain knowledge that I *know* what I'm talking and writing about this time.

MOTOR SPORT, *July, 1955*

MILLE MIGLIA 1955 RESULTS		
1ST	Stirling Moss	Mercedes-Benz 97.95 mph average
2ND	J. M. Fangio	Mercedes-Benz
3RD	U. Maglioli	Ferrari

CHAPTER TEN:

The honor of winning the fastest race ever run anywhere in the world goes to an American, Jim Rathmann, one of the great track drivers of all time. The car was a Zink Leader Card Special, built by A. J. Watson. The overall speed for three heats totaling 500 miles was 166.72 mph. And the place, the Monza autodrome in northern Italy.

A great deal more than three thousand miles of ocean separates American from European motor racing. In Europe most motor racing is run on roads, either public roads

FASTEST RACE EVER –

closed for the occasion or tracks specially built to seem like roads. For this reason the problems of balance and springing of the cars have always been more acute in Europe, where drivers may have to cope with every kind of corner, road surface, and even gradient. In addition, the rules, or formula, governing the construction of Grand Prix cars usually limit the engine to a smaller size than is usual in American racing.

The gap between European and American racing

191

practice has steadily narrowed during the past ten or fif-
teen years with the growth in popularity of European
sports cars and European-style road racing in America.
But American track racing, with events all over the nation
and once annually, of course, at Indianapolis, is still very
different in every way from European Grand Prix racing.

In 1957 there occurred an interesting experiment,
however. The Italian race authorities invited over the best
of cars and drivers American track racing had to offer for
an Indianapolis-style 500-mile race at Monza, the fastest
specially-constructed track racing circuit in the world,
normally used only for record breaking and testing. The
race was officially named the "500 Miglia di Monza." The
Americans cleaned up the prize money, the winner being
Jimmy Bryan—who won while smoking a cigar—to the
delight of the crowds.

In 1958 this exciting and very fast race was repeated.
The European racing-car constructors had nothing to
offer that could seriously hope to compete with the

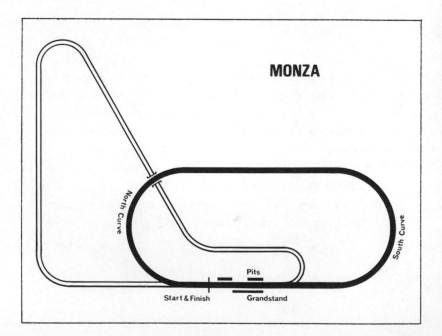

MONZA

North Curve

South Curve

Pits

Start & Finish   Grandstand

Americans, whose Offenhauser-engined machines had been brought to a high pitch of sophistication and perfection by years of experience in track racing. But at least this year much of the prejudice against the race felt in 1957 by European drivers and manufacturers had now gone, and Ferrari, Maserati, and Jaguar were among those whose cars appeared for battle against the all-conquering Americans.

Enzo Ferrari's men produced a 4.1-liter V12 for Italian champion Luigi Musso and a 3-liter for Phil Hill. The Maserati works put together a huge 4.1 liter car for Stirling Moss. And there were Jaguar-engined cars for Ivor Bueb, Jack Fairman, and American Masten Gregory, although it was known that none of these could hope to catch the Indianapolis cars. Of the Americans, Jimmy Bryan was back this year with a Belond A. P.; Tony Ruttman had the Aganjanian Special; Veith, the Bowes Seal Fast; and Rathmann, of course, the Zink Leader Card.

The 1958 Miglia di Monza was much more than a very exciting motor race and the fastest ever run anywhere in the world. It brought together the bright colors, cheerful professionalism, and the breezy courage of the American track-racing scene with the stiffer, more conservative, and clublike atmosphere that marks European motor racing. Both sides benefited from the friendly exchange. The European teams certainly learned how ruthless and cut-and-thrust is the American style of racing; and the American drivers learned, from the performance of Luigi Musso and Stirling Moss alone, that the European driver can quickly adapt himself to the higher speeds and different style of track racing when it is demanded of him.

193

Of the other European drivers mentioned in this account by Denis Jenkinson, Mike Hawthorn was World Champion driver for 1958, Maurice Trintignant was French Champion, and Harry Schell a somewhat elderly (for motor racing) and most charming Franco-American.

THE CHIEF CONTESTANTS	
DRIVERS	CARS
J. Rathmann (U.S.A.)	Zink Leader Card Special (U.S.A.)
J. Bryan (U.S.A.)	Belond A.P. Special (U.S.A.)
L. Musso (Italy)	Ferrari 4.1 liters (Italy)
S. Moss (Britain)	Eldorado-Maserati (Italy)

1958 *MIGLIA DI MONZA*

BY DENIS JENKINSON

On race day the weather was really hot and the race was arranged to be run in three separate heats of 63 laps each, with 1½ hours between heats, during which time the cars would be worked on as required. There were nineteen entries in all—ten American track drivers in Indianapolis

194

cars and nine European and American road-racing drivers
in a motley collection of cars from Italy, Britain, and
America. The order of lining up on the starting grid for
the first heat was in accordance with the qualifying times
set up in practice, and it was a very proud Musso who sat
among the Americans on the front row with the big red
Ferrari 4.1 liter. A rolling start was used behind a vast
white Ford Fairlane. The cars went around the opening
laps paired in the following order:

Veith
(Bowes Seal Fast)

Musso
(Ferrari 4.1 liters)

Sachs
(Jim Robbins Special)

Fangio
(Dean Van Lines) nonstarter

Bryan
(Belond A.P. Special)

Freeland
(Bob Estes)

Thomson
(D.A. Lubricant)

Rathmann
(Zink Leader Card)

Ruttman
(Agajanian Special)

Ward
(Wolcott Fuel Injection)

Crawford
(Meguiar's Mirror Glaze)

Moss
(Eldorado-Maserati)

Hill
(Ferrari V-6)

Reece
(Hoyt Machine)

Gregory
(Jaguar D)

Trintignant
(Scalvi & Amos)

Schell
(Ferrari 4.1 liters)

Fairman
(Lister-Jaguar)

Bueb
(Jaguar D)

They appeared in sight low on the north banking, still in formation, traveling at about 80 mph.

As the flag fell it was the red Ferrari that shot off into the lead, and Musso screamed it around the very top of the banking, leaving the Americans wondering which way he had gone. On lap 1 the Ferrari was well ahead, followed by Sachs, Rathmann, Bryan, and Freeland, with Phil Hill on the smaller Ferrari leading Veith, Thomson, and Moss. This was what everyone had been longing to see, for the European cars were making the Indianapolis boys hurry along. On lap 3 Sachs got up alongside Musso and they ran wheel to wheel at well over 170 mph, neither giving way, while Rathmann was close behind, followed by Bryan and Freeland. On lap 4 Musso was still leading, but on the next lap Sachs took the lead. The gallant Italian driver did not give up, and he fought Sachs and Rathmann as hard as they fought him, so that these three drew away from the rest of the field. On lap 8 Rathmann took the lead, and on the following lap the three came off the north banking in a close bunch. There was a pack of slower cars passing the pits, traveling at a mere 160 mph, and the three leaders went through this lot without lifting off, so for a brief moment the wide Monza track seemed full of cars and it was almost impossible to see where they all went. There was passing on right and left, and Musso went right down the pit area, a few feet from the wall, scattering mechanics and marshals, but determined not to lose contact with Sachs and Rathmann, who were weaving their way through the cars in the center of the track. Somehow all three got through and it was Musso who led once more as they went round the south banking, but in the next lap Rathmann was back in the lead.

This may not have been Grand Prix racing, but it was motor racing and there was no quarter being given, for the race average was close to 170 mph. Meanwhile Bryan and Freeland were still in very close company in the Belond and the Bob Estes, the two yellow cars seemingly very evenly matched. Farther back Moss was keeping the Eldorado-Maserati on the tails of the cars of Ward and Veith, but Hill had dropped out with a defective magneto on the V-6 Dino-engined Ferrari 3 liter. Rathmann took the lead on lap 11 and though he maintained it after that, he still had the bright red Ferrari and the dark red Jim Robbins Special very close behind him, and on lap 17 Sachs got his car right up alongside Rathmann in a do-or-die attempt to get the lead, but it was no good. The Zink car was too good and on lap 20 Sachs coasted into the pits with a connecting rod sticking out of the side of the engine on the Jim Robbins car.

Meanwhile Musso had worn himself out completely, for he had not been in a very fit state before the event, and fighting the uncontrollable Ferrari around the bankings was more than anyone could hope to do for very long at the speed he was going. He had done a wonderful job and really shaken the Indianapolis drivers, but now his race was run and he dropped back into second place, making despairing signs of fatigue as he passed the pits. Behind him Bryan was running the Belond Special comfortably in third place, for Freeland had overstretched the Bob Estes Special and a camshaft drive had broken, while there was more trouble further back when Ward retired with a broken chassis and split exhaust manifold, leaving Moss ahead of Veith in fourth and fifth positions, but a long way behind the leader. However, for sixth place there was still a strong battle waging between Ruttman and Thomson, these two having been wheel to wheel since the beginning of the race.

On lap 26 it was all over, for Musso could go no longer and he drew into the pits, staggered from the car, and slumped on the pit counter, completely spent after a truly heroic fight. The Firestone tires on the car were getting badly scrubbed due to the sliding round the bankings, so all four were changed and it was found that the spokes in the rear wheels were breaking up. This stop let Bryan into second place but not close enough to challenge the leader, and it also brought Moss up into third place, the big Maserati now rumbling around very regularly.

Hawthorn took over the Ferrari, but there was not the enthusiasm in the English driver that there had been in the Italian, and it did not look to be the same car, cruising around at the back of the fast cars and not making any ground on them, which was a pity after Musso's valiant efforts in the opening stages. Hawthorn was not right at the back, for Reece, Trintignant, Crawford, Fairman, Schell, and Bueb were tailing along many laps behind the leader. Like many a European event the race settled into a procession between laps 27 and 47, with Rathmann circulating a comfortable 10 to 15 seconds ahead of Bryan, and both a lap ahead of Moss, Veith, Ruttman and Thomson. Next came Hawthorn, and on lap 43 Moss lapped the big Ferrari and for a time the two European drivers ran side by side. Moss slowed a little, so that Veith began to close up on him. Half a lap away the leader was about to lap Ruttman in the Agajanian Special, who was a little ahead of Thomson in the D.A. Lubricant car.

Between laps 43 and 57 there was a fine object lesson

in track racing, for Jim Rathmann was lapping faster than all the others and as he lapped the Agajanian Special Ruttman got into his slipstream and hung on to the Zink Leader Card car. This maneuver got him away from Thomson, with whom he had been racing since the beginning, and towed him nearer and nearer to Moss and Veith. He had been lapping at the same speed as they, and now this tow in the slipstream of the Zink car was bringing him closer to them. Meanwhile, due to lack of concentration and running in company with Hawthorn, whom he had just lapped, Moss lost third place, for Veith went by while he was not looking. On lap 52 the leader caught up with Moss again and Ruttman went by with him, taking fourth place from the Maserati. On lap 57 the same maneuver happened with Veith, so that Ruttman was now third, having got in the slipstream of the leader while in fifth place.

This very clever piece of track driving was all wasted in the next lap, for the car ran short of fuel. Ruttman stopped at his pit and he fell back to seventh place. Jim Rathmann, looking remarkably comfortable and untroubled, completed the 63 laps at an average speed of 167.28 mph, and he was followed by Bryan, Veith, Moss, Thomson, Hawthorn, Ruttman and the rest, fourteen of the eighteen starters still being in at the end of the first heat. Out for good were Sachs, Freeland, and Hill, while Ward was able to repair the Wolcott Fuel-Injection car in time for heat 2.

After an interval the cars lined up in pairs again in the order in which they had finished heat 1, this time behind a Lancia Spyder driven by Villoresi. The Ferrari was still going perfectly and Musso took over again, while A. J. Foyt replaced Trintingnant in the Scalvi & Amos

car. The pairs of drivers were in this order: Rathmann/
Bryan, Veith/Moss, Thomson/Musso, Ruttman/Reece,
Foyt/Crawford, Fairman/Schell, Gregory/Bueb. This
time Musso could not hope to get into the lead from the
third row of the rolling start. Rathmann had no trouble
at all in this heat, and after only 3 laps he had drawn out
a comfortable lead. But for second place it was a different
story.

No matter what anyone might say about track racing, there is no denying the fact that the racing can be so
close at times that the cars are almost touching. Veith,
Musso, Bryan, and Moss were nose to tail for second place
and the pace was hot, so much so that after a while Bryan
dropped back, leaving Veith to battle against the two Eu-
ropeans. Quite clearly Moss realized that anything Musso
could do, he could do better, and the Maserati was a far
better track car than the Ferrari. Lapping at 57 seconds
(167 mph) the Ferrari and the Maserati really had a go
at putting the Bowes Seal Fast Special in its place, but
Veith eventually got the better of them and after 12 laps
began to draw ahead. Meanwhile Bryan was being harried
by Ruttman, and Foyt was not far behind. Musso became
exhausted once more and gradually dropped back. Moss
was content to settle for third place, and after 19 laps the
Ferrari stopped at the pits for new tires, and this time
Phil Hill took over. At 20 laps the order was Rathmann,
Veith, Moss, Ruttman, Bryan, and Foyt, the rest of the
runners having been lapped by the leader, though Hill was
now traveling fast and making up time for the Ferrari's
pit stop.

On lap 24 a new Stirling Moss began to appear and
for the next twenty-one laps one saw the wonderful sight of

a truly great driver allowing his inner self and inborn skill and courage to take full command and throw off the worry and fright that he had allowed to build up around him prior to this race. It all started when Ruttman went past. Moss had seen him try to drive a sports car at Sebring in the past and to be overtaken by an inferior driver was more than he could stand. He opened out the Maserati V-8 engine and regained his lead, but then Bryan went by and at that point Moss realized that you did not have to be a big hairy man to race against these Indianapolis boys; little Stirling Moss with skill and courage was quite sufficient. He then started to mix it really close with Bryan and Ruttman and as they lapped the slower cars he followed them through impossible gaps and sat right in their slipstreams around the bankings.

Musso in the big Ferrari (No. 12) holds Jimmy Bryan
at 170 mph on the straight.
AUTOMOBILE YEAR PHOTO

This three-cornered dogfight was going on at lap speeds of 168 mph, almost the same speed as the leader Rathmann was circulating at, and for lap after lap Moss battled away against the two big Americans, both these drivers' physical stature making even Mike Hawthorn look quite small when they all stood together. The Maserati was a match for both the Belond and the Agajanian Specials and there was never more than a few feet between the three cars. Moss discovered that in track racing it was every man for himself. You did not move over and let your rival through; if he wanted to get by he had to find a way by, and you raced as close as you could, even to the point of interlocking wheels if necessary. It was tough and rough. The real Stirling Moss had suddenly realized that he could play it that way, and Bryan and Ruttman were made to sweat it out.

During the twenty-one laps of this wonderful display of hard racing, with all three really pushing each other, they had numerous occasions on which they had to lap groups of slower cars, and at one time Foyt, Reece, and Crawford were passing the pits and about to lap Fairman in the Lister-Jaguar, when *woosh!* the Belond, the Maserati, and the Agajanian swept through them on all sides and there was the incredible sight of seven cars all traveling between 160 and 175 mph in a solid bunch, heading for the narrow banking, with poor Jack Fairman completely surrounded by thundering great track cars. If anyone had the impression that Monza racing was dull they should have seen just that one sight, while similar things were happening all around the track.

Meanwhile Rathmann was sailing around in the lead, having twice received the "slow" sign from his pit, to which he replied with a despairing gesture that indicated "but I am going slow"—he was still lapping at over 165 mph. On lap 55 Moss was still between his two American rivals, but he then saw that one of the rear tires was nearly worn right through, so he reluctantly had to ease up and let them go for the remaining few laps, but it had been a memorable race for third position. Hill had been driving the Ferrari hard and fast and he got up to seventh position only to have to make another stop for tires, losing two positions in the meantime. Had the race gone on for another lap, he would have regained his position. Eleven cars finished this second heat, and the winner's speed was down on heat 1, being 165.52 mph, but nevertheless much faster than the previous year's race. Veith, Bryan, and Ruttman finished on the same lap as the leader, in that order, with Moss fifth, Foyt sixth, and Reece, Crawford, Hill, Fairman, and Bueb following in that order. Three cars gave up for good: Thomson with a broken crankshaft, Ward with a broken chassis frame, and Schell with "mechanical boredom." Fairman blew up in a big way as he crossed the line, so that though he was classed as a finisher, he could race no more.

After another interval, during which the Ferrari needed nothing done to it at all in the way of repairs, the cars lined up for heat 3. The line-up was Rathmann/Veith, Bryan/Ruttman, Moss/Foyt, Reece/Crawford, Hawthorn (in the Ferrari) with a space beside him that should have been Fairman, Bueb/Gregory, and Fangio bringing up the rear. When everyone had got his engine running the pace car set off and the field trickled off after it, all, that is, except Moss, for the Maserati was giving trouble getting into gear. This was a pity, for Moss was all set for another battle against the leading American drivers. This trouble at the getaway lost him nearly half a lap, for the field were rolling and the start was given as they reappeared down past the pits. With no European cars near the front, Rathmann, Bryan, and Veith got stuck in a close battle on their own, and for the next 18 laps the spectators had a perfect exhibition of high-speed track racing. These three drivers knew each other well so that each had to try and pull out something new in order to gain an advantage, but Rathmann was first across the line every time. As there was a prize of some £30 for the leader on every lap throughout the race, Veith and Bryan were trying hard to wrest some of the money from Rathmann. They were lapping consistently at more than 171 mph, sometimes ending the lap in line-ahead formation, other times almost line abreast, but always Rathmann had the advantage by a few inches. The average speed rose to 172½ mph and for one happy moment Bryan led the race on lap 18 and collected £30 for his efforts, but that was the only time, for Rathmann was back there ticking up the thirty quid every time around.

This battle rather overshadowed the rest of the runners, such as Crawford and Reece, while Moss was making up for his bad start and this time stormed past Hawthorn and did not wait to say anything to him. The Maserati was lapped steadily at 165 mph, which was impressive enough in itself, but to see the three leaders lap Moss on the north banking as if he were a rabbit at the end of the field was quite remarkable.

After 24 laps Hawthorn stopped for a change of the left front tire and Phil Hill took over and made the Ferrari rush along, though it was 400 rpm down since the be-

CHAPTER ELEVEN:

A long time ago, just after the end of World War II, when money and resources for building new racing automobiles were both in short supply, a young British engineer named John Cooper carried out an ingenious and interesting experiment. He took two diminutive Fiat 500 stock sedans, sawed off the front of each of the chassis, and welded the two front ends together. Then he fixed a single-cylinder engine over the rear axle and built a thin alloy body around the driver's cockpit. It was ridiculously small and

FASTEST FORD IN THE WORLD

comical. But it was so light that it accelerated like a rocket and so well balanced that it held the road like a limpet.

This little car, and others like it, was so successful that a new class of racing for up-and-coming drivers with little money to spend on their machines was started. It was called 500 cc.-class racing, and all the cars had to have engines with a cylinder capacity not exceeding half a liter. A number of engineers built cars for this class of racing, but for the ten years or so that it lasted, the Cooper,

*Forerunner of the modern lightweight rear-engined race car
was this little Cooper, seen here at Le Mans.*

*usually with a Norton motorcycle engine, almost always
dominated the field. Stirling Moss was only one of many
drivers who were to test and demonstrate their early skill
on these machines.*

*But the Cooper 500 was only the beginning of an
engineering saga that has changed the face of motor racing
in Europe. We shall see shortly that the same principles
applied by John Cooper in 1946 are changing the face of
American racing in the mid-1960s. Cooper built numerous
other sports and racing sports cars during the 1940s and
1950s. Most were rear-engined and nearly all of them were
successful in their class. But Formula 1 Grand Prix racing
still seemed too fast and too rugged to be considered for
his lithe little machines; they seemed to be mere toys compared with the massive 180 mph Mercedes-Benz, Ferrari,
Maserati, Gordini, and Vanwall 2½-liter racing cars.
Then in the 1957 season a cheeky young Australian*

210

named Jack Brabham took the daring step of entering his little Formula 2 Cooper racing car, with slightly enlarged engine, in a full scale Grand Prix. It aroused a great deal of laughter when it appeared at Monte Carlo for the Monaco Grand Prix. But it went around the hairpin corners of this round-the-houses race at a remarkable speed, and to everyone's astonishment was running third near the end. It failed to finish only because of a trivial fault.

For the rest of that 1957 season, more rear-engined Coopers made their appearance in Grands Prix, and better-informed observers began to recognize that they might one day be a real threat to the traditional big front engined-rear-driven Formula 1 racing cars. At Pescara and in the French Grand Prix, Brabham was seventh, and it was noticed how the delicate balance of the car, provided by the advanced understanding of geometry and spring-loadings and weight distribution possessed by John Cooper's engineers, gave the Cooper a great advantage on every corner—an advantage that could not always be made up by the superior power of the traditional cars on the straights.

That winter, one driver in particular began to give a lot of thought to the likely change in the motor racing scene. This was Stirling Moss. A few months later, Moss caused a sensation when he appeared at the opening event of 1958 at Buenos Aires in a Cooper, sponsored by the Scotch whiskey millionaire Rob Walker. It was a very different and much more complicated machine than the 500 in which he had won innumerable races some ten years earlier. But the basic principles were the same. These were fine balance and high power to weight ratio obtained by putting a comparatively simple and reliable engine behind

211

the driver and in a featherweight tubular framework. The engine in this car, built by Coventry-Climax, manufacturers of stationary pump engines for many years, was less than 2 liters, producing 170 horsepower. This was more than 100 horsepower less than the 2½-liter Ferraris. But by running on one set of tires throughout the race—made possible by the lightness of his machine—Moss kept ahead of all the Ferraris and Maseratis and won by just 2½ seconds after more than two hours of racing.

This race marked the real breakthrough for the rear-engined lightweight Grand Prix car in European racing. By the end of 1958 every manufacturer recognized that John Cooper's genius had brought about a revolution—a triumph of engineering subtlety over brute force. Cooper won the World Championship in 1959 and 1960, and the traditional heavy front-engined racing car was dead.

Now to move forward a few more years. One of John Cooper's keenest observers and admirers has always been the Londoner Colin Chapman, who was building highly effective sports and racing sports cars in the early 1950s. He, too, believed in weight-saving wherever it could be obtained, in making every component not only as light as possible but capable of at least two functions. His first Grand Prix cars were fielded in 1957. They were very light and held the road as well as the Coopers, but they were too frail. The handicap of unreliability dogged the Lotus* Grand Prix cars for several years. And it was not until

---

* How did Colin Chapman's Lotus get its curious name? It is said that he christened his first car Lotus after the blossom that induces drowsiness because his men were overcome with the need to sleep after working all night to make it ready for its first event. (*Ed.*)

Colin Chapman followed his rival John Cooper by placing the engine behind the driver that he could match the best that Europe had to offer.

By 1962 Lotus was offering the next stage in weight-saving ingenuity, a "monocoque" stressed-aluminum chassis in which the body and chassis of the machine were in effect no more than a single shell, with the engine, transmission, and suspension attached to a steel sub-frame. Now there were not even fuel tanks; instead, the 32 imperial gallons of fuel were carried in flexible rubberized bags in order to shave more weight. And the driver lay almost flat on his back to cut wind resistance. After the initial bugs were sorted out, this car, the Lotus 25, proved unbeatable in Grand Prix racing.

Meanwhile, murmurs of the engineering upheavals in European racing were beginning to filter through to the ultraconservative confines of the Indianapolis brickyard. Back in the early days of the "500," European influence had been felt, and the French firm of Peugeot, among others, had successes there. Then again, after a long period of supremacy by Duesenberg, Miller, and others, Grand Prix Maseratis, by their victories at Indianapolis in 1939 and 1940, began a "new look" in American racing, started by Frank Curtis and perpetuated by A. J. Watson.

But by the early 1960s, engineering sterility, in the form of the Offenhauser, Meyer-Drake and V-8 Novi engines in particular, had settled its heavy hand over the brickyard. The cars were immensely fast and reliable, as the traditional Ferraris, Maseratis, and Vanwalls had been in Europe before the Cooper revolution. But they were heavy and by Lotus and Cooper terms, inefficient.

Dan Gurney was among many who recognized the

reality of the state of affairs at Indianapolis. He was in a strong position to do so. He had raced for several years in Europe in most types of cars. In 1962 at Indianapolis he drove a car with a rear-mounted Buick V-8 engine, and this experience made him realize the potential of light-

The old order and the new order. Here, side by side at Indianapolis, are (LEFT) Rodger Ward and his mechanic, A. J. Watson, and (RIGHT) Colin Chapman, designer of the Lotus-Ford, with Dan Gurney at the wheel.
INDIANAPOLIS MOTOR SPEEDWAY PHOTO

weight European-style racing cars in the American classic.

Later in the year Gurney invited Colin Chapman over to the United States. From this meeting and later discussions with the Engine Division of the Ford Motor Company in Detroit, Chapman devised a slightly enlarged version of his Lotus 25 Grand Prix car, powered by a rear-mounted 4.2-liter V-8 Ford engine. Ford offered every sort of cooperation. They were even prepared to produce a more elaborated twin-overhead camshaft engine, with fuel injection and running on alcohol. But in accordance with his beliefs, Chapman chose simplicity, and Ford made for him three modified aluminum Fairlane engines with Weber carburetors which comfortably met the requirement of providing one bhp for each pound of weight—370 bhp in all. This was a good deal less than the traditional Indianapolis engines provided, but the Lotus was much smaller and lighter than its American counterparts, and Chapman calculated that not only would he get through the Indy turns faster, but he could run through the 500 miles with one less pit stop—a vital factor in this race.

Three of these Ford-engined Lotuses, called the Lotus 29, were built at Colin Chapman's plant at Cheshunt, among the beech woods of the Chiltern Hills northwest of London. They were by far the most powerful and fastest cars ever made there. After much testing, the second two followed the prototype to the United States. Dan Gurney himself and Jim Clark—Scottish farmer, Lotus number one driver, and 1963 World Champion driver—were nominated to drive.

You can read the result of this Lotus-powered-by-Ford invasion in the following brief account of the race first published in Sports Illustrated *magazine. It was an*

215

*Jim Clark, Scottish farmer and 1963 World Champion,
at the helm of the lightweight rear-engined Lotus-Ford.*
INDIANAPOLIS MOTOR SPEEDWAY PHOTO

*epochal race—perhaps the most momentous ever run at the
brickyard. Colin Chapman's second place was as important to American racing as Stirling Moss's victory in the
first Grand Prix of 1958 was to European racing. Both
represented the belated but final acceptance of the new
order, and both demonstrated once again that in the long
history of engineering, progress can never cease and that
conservatism is the negation of the highest philosophy of
engineering development.*

THE CHIEF CONTESTANTS	
DRIVERS	CARS
R. Parnelli Jones *(U.S.A.)*	Willard Battery Special 4.2 liters *(American)*
Jim Clark *(Britain)*	Lotus-Ford 3.7 liters *(Anglo-American)*
Dan Gurney *(U.S.A.)*	Lotus-Ford 3.7 liters *(Anglo-American)*
A. J. Foyt *(U.S.A.)*	Sheraton-Thompson Special 4.2 liters *(American)*
Rodger Ward *(U.S.A.)*	Kaiser Aluminum Special 4.2 liters *(American)*

1963 INDIANAPOLIS 500

BY KENNETH RUDEEN

The perils of Parnelli Jones are among the enduring fascinations of auto racing. Two years ago the hard-muscled, chain-smoking Californian made the Indianapolis 500-mile race for the first time—and was smacked in the face by a rock flipped back by the tire of an opponent's car. Last year he became the first driver ever to lap the old Hoosier speedway at 150 miles per hour and was uncatchable in the race itself—until his brakes failed.

Last week, in the most heavily attended, richest, fast-

217

est and possibly most exciting "500" of all, Parnelli outdid himself. First he nearly ran out of fuel, then he was pressed to use all his famous foot to repulse the insurgent Lotus-Fords, and finally he raced the closing laps in urgent danger of being flagged off to defeat because his pearl-grey Offenhauser roadster was leaking oil.

But this time the finish was strictly from Sunset and Vine. It was Parnelli for whom the checkered flag dipped first, Parnelli who collected the winner's $148,513 share of the most lavish purse in sport—a total of $493,530—to divide with his car owner, J. C. Agajanian, and his chief mechanic, Johnny Pouelsen.

On the following day Parnelli won another decision. Eddie Sachs, a very fine but very emotional driver who had spun, restarted, and later lost a wheel toward the race's end, had been telling everyone he met that Parnelli's oil leak had "jeopardized the lives of every driver on the track," and that Parnelli therefore "was not a good win-

The motor racing scene is ever changing, and as Jim Clark
prepares to go by Don Branson the great Indianapolis
crowd is witnessing the beginning of a design revolution.
INDIANAPOLIS MOTOR SPEEDWAY PHOTO

ner." He met Parnelli himself at a luncheon. Words flew, then Parnelli's heavy right fist. Sachs was hit solidly on the mouth. The drivers grappled and were separated before more punches could be thrown. Adding to Sachs's woes, Harlan Fengler, chief steward of the "500," fined him $100 for failing to make a precautionary pit stop after his spinout.

It was exceedingly difficult to sympathize with Sachs. Running fourth and no threat to the leaders when he spun, he emerged as a distraction to the "500's" spectacular main theme—a duel between Parnelli in his thoroughly orthodox Offy and Scotland's Jimmy Clark in one of the Lotus-Fords.

The huge crowd of some 225,000 persons had been in continuous uproar when Clark held the lead for 27 laps in mid-race, with his American stablemate Dan Gurney tailgating in second place for much of that span. The situation with 162 of the race's 200 laps completed was still

more electric. Parnelli pitted for the third time for fuel and a change of tires, and after a neat 21.1-second job by his mechanics emerged only 11 seconds ahead of Clark, who had made one stop and would require no more. In a magnificent stern chase Clark cut Parnelli's advantage to 4½ seconds at 178 laps.

Then, in swift and puzzling sequence, Sachs spun, Parnelli's car commenced to trail ominous black smoke and Clark fell back, ultimately finishing 34 seconds behind Parnelli. Alarmingly, Drivers Roger McCluskey and Bobby Marshman spun out on Parnelli's very last lap. McCluskey, in third place before the mishap, which cost him some $25,000, angrily charged that Parnelli's car was "dumping" oil, had been for "30 or 40 laps," and should have been black-flagged.

Colin Chapman, British builder of the Lotus-Ford chassis, said: "At the end Parnelli Jones's car was pouring oil out. Three cars spun on it. The whole race slowed down 5 mph."

Jimmy Clark said: "I had enough rubber and petrol to go as fast as before, but I was getting sideways on Parnelli Jones's oil. I thought I'd try to keep my car on the island. I would much rather be second than dead."

But Chapman and Clark sportingly gave Parnelli congratulatory handshakes for his victory. Chapman's final words were generous. "I must admit," he said, "that I would have been very sorry to see Parnelli Jones black-flagged."

The responsibility for deciding whether or not to use the black flag, which requires a driver to come into the pits for consultation, lay with Chief Steward Fengler. He later explained why he had permitted Parnelli to finish.

"I could see that oil was spewing from Parnelli's car and I wanted to know the reason. I told the starter to get the black flag ready. I sent for Agajanian and Pouelsen. Pouelsen told me there was nothing the matter with the car's engine; the oil was coming from the tank on the outside of the car. I went close to the track to observe. In my opinion, the oil had stopped spewing. I could see that the car's tire treads were dry, so obviously no oil was spraying directly onto them.

"There is no question that the car put a certain amount of oil on the track. So did other cars in one degree or another. It is part of the race; it always happens. If I had thought Parnelli was creating hazardous conditions, I would have had him black-flagged."

Johnny Pouelsen, understandably, was in complete agreement. "There is oil on the track wherever we race," he said. "Parnelli's tank had 21 quarts of oil in it when he started and still had 12 quarts when he finished. He could hardly have been coating the track with oil."

The oil was coming from a tiny 3/8-inch crack at the forward bolt that helps to anchor Parnelli's streamlined, tear-shaped outboard tank to his car. When the oil spray struck the car's fiery-hot exhaust pipe it created plumes of smoke. "When I saw that you were smoking," Clark told Parnelli with a grin on his boyish face and a twinkle in his eye, "I thought, 'Aha! You won't last until the end now.' "

It would have been a shame if he had not—and a shame, too, if Fengler had flagged him off. Unquestionably, Fengler was on a very hot spot. He presumably would have black-flagged the Jones car if it had been out of serious contention. Fengler is an ex-racing driver, however, knowing better than most how greatly the Indy men strive to win this loftiest of American racing prizes, and his every impulse must have been to give the leader the widest latitude.

By calling Parnelli in, Fengler would have summarily handed the race to Clark. There was glory enough for the little Grand Prix driver and Lotus-Fords. The fact that would be remembered after the oil squabble had dimmed was that it took the most strenuous exertions of the most nearly perfect "500" driver of modern times—Rufus Parnell Jones—to defeat them.

If there was a matter for regret, it was that conditions did not permit Clark to continue his remarkable late-race pursuit of Parnelli and perhaps actually race wheel to wheel with him. Parnelli said he could not see his pit signals very well and did not realize how quickly Clark's yellow-striped green bullet was overtaking him. Logic says Parnelli would have won in *mano a mano* combat; he had invariably been faster than Clark in practice. Still, with his blood up, racing a handy car that made the heavier Offenhausers look like tractors in the turns, thumping some of the very fastest Offies despite their ability to outdrag him leaving the turns, Clark would have made the finish unforgettably close.

What's more, there was fuel for a thousand arguments in Parnelli's shrewd and fortunate use of yellow caution lights—by making his second and third pit stops while they were on, and by increasing his advantage over Clark, at times, while running under them.

Green lights around the track go out and yellow ones on when an accident occurs. Last week the yellows were on for an unusually long time—48 minutes 38 seconds of the race's 3½ hours—as nine drivers spun, hit walls or had mechanical failures requiring workmen to clear the track.

Under the yellow the racing pace is supposed to slow to 120 mph and drivers are not supposed to improve their positions. This never works out very tidily. One driver's estimated 120 is actually 120 mph and another's 110. Some cars benefit, others suffer. Last week Jones clearly benefited—by how much is conjecture.

"I think," said Clark, "that I lost at least a minute on yellow lights. In the middle of the race I was stuck behind a fellow who wouldn't get going and I was losing three seconds a lap to Parnelli."

"Our experience under the yellow lights," said Colin Chapman, "dropped us just that little bit and cost us the race."

Maybe so, maybe not. "If" questions like this can never be satisfactorily answered, because a race obviously cannot be rerun—with wrongs righted—from the point at which controversy develops.

Parnelli had a pretty big if of his own. "If," he said, "we hadn't goofed by not taking on quite enough fuel at the start, I could have run the race on two pit stops instead of three and then nobody could have made it close. To get by on two stops I knew I had to make close to 70 laps on my first tank. I had to come in after only 63, and at that my engine nearly died in the pits. Then I knew I was committed to three stops."

About another important matter, however, there is no if at all. Clark gained much by making only one pit stop but lost a number of precious seconds because that stop was not up to Indy's high standards. Twenty seconds is excellent, 25 not bad, but the 32-plus expended by Clark's crewmen was mediocre. Worse was the 42.2-second job for

Where tenths of seconds count!
Jim Clark pits at the 1963 Indianapolis.

INDIANAPOLIS MOTOR SPEEDWAY PHOTO

The last of the "heavy metal," American style and European style.
Parnelli Jones, 1963 Indianapolis winner,
in his Willard Battery Special.
INDIANAPOLIS MOTOR SPEEDWAY PHOTO

Gurney when he pulled in a few laps earlier. This was perhaps to be expected of a group tackling the "500" for the first time; the future should bring sharp improvement.

Followers of racing had been kicking a good many ifs around for weeks—and a good thing, too, because the only real question to be settled during the past decade at Indy was which Offenhauser roadster would win.

This year there was spectacular novelty. First, and most promising, there were the nimble, frameless Lotuses with chassis by Chapman and rear-mounted V-8 aluminum engines, made by the Ford Motor Company, which burned pump gasoline, not the usual racing alcohol. California's indefatigable Mickey Thompson, a man who feels guilty if he sleeps more than three hours a night, entered five Chev-

Stirling Moss, 1958 Italian Grand Prix winner,
at the pits in his Vanwall.

rolet-engined V-8s. A startlingly low, wide new model was qualified by veteran Duane Carter, at 50 the oldest of the drivers in the race. Its engine blew. A 1962 Thompson car was qualified by an unknown Indy rookie, 39-year-old Al Miller. It finished ninth. With General Motors on an anti-racing binge, Thompson was denied the Chevrolet financial backing he might have been able to count on in other years. He seemed to be attempting too much too late on too thin a pocketbook.

Then there were the Novis—lovable, wailing, super-charged brutes which, since their first "500" appearance in 1941, had created a body of fans as deliriously faithful —and unrewarded—as those of the New York Mets. As-tonishingly, three Novis made the 33-car starting field, with one driven by leadfoot Jim Hurtubise smack in the front row. One spun out in the second lap, another never really got going, but Hurtubise at least had the satisfaction of leading the first lap. His Novi, unfortunately, broke down in mid-race.

These intruders left 26 places for the conventional roadsters, and besides Parnelli such formidable drivers as former winners Rodger Ward, A. J. Foyt, Jim Rathmann and Troy Ruttman (who won the race in an Agajanian car in 1952).

Indianapolis pulsed with anticipation the night before the race. Thousands shivered through the chilly hours in and around their cars, ringing the speedway, and raced for the best infield viewing spots when the gates opened at 5 A.M.; as less impulsive racegoers drove in Thursday they saw a few flaked out, fast asleep, in bunkers of the golf course that is part of the vast infield.

Aerial bombs exploded, colorful balloons floated into the cloudless sky, Astronaut Gordon Cooper made one orbit of the track with Speedway Owner Tony Hulman, to ecstatic applause, and then at 11 o'clock, the "500" was rousingly, noisily on.

The race evolved in three distinct parts. From his starting position on the pole, Parnelli swooped away to an impressive lead. When he pitted first, his margin was half a minute, or approximately half a lap.

Always with the fastest flight of a dozen cars in the first phase, the Lotus-Fords of Clark and Gurney starred in the second segment, as they ran one, two. Distressingly, Gurney was not getting enough wear from his right rear tire to make the one-stop race both he and Clark had planned. He had to get new rubber after 92 laps, and knew then he could not win. "It took the heart out of me," he said later. "We didn't get the riggin' of Dan's car right," Chapman said. Thus another if: Gurney might well have joined Clark in that marvelous stern chase of Parnelli. Ultimately, however, he pitted again after 183 laps—and again one lap later to have a loose wheel tightened. Despite these misadventures he managed to place seventh.

When Clark made his pit stop Parnelli recaptured the lead and never again lost it. He earned every decibel of the ovation given him. And, just as surely, he knew that his might have been the last triumphant stand of the now out-moded roadster. New, smaller, fatter 15-inch tires of the kind used on the Lotus-Fords gave the Offies decidedly better wear than their old 18-inch rear and 16-inch front tires. Now most Offies should drive the "500" on only two stops. But two should be one too many.

"The old cars," said Miamian Lindsey Hopkins, long an owner of "500" roadsters, "have got to go."

First published under the title
"Close Call for a Jones Boy"
in SPORTS ILLUSTRATED, *June 10, 1963,*
and reproduced by permission of
the publisher, Time, Inc.

INDIANAPOLIS 500 MILE 1963 RESULTS		
1ST	R. Parnelli Jones	Willard Battery Special 143.137 mph average
2ND	Jim Clark	Lotus-Ford
3RD	A. J. Foyt	Sheraton-Thompson Special

ABOUT THE EDITOR

Racing journalist, children's book editor, naval historian, and writer of books for young people, Richard Hough was born in Brighton, England, and educated at Frensham Heights. During World War II he served as a fighter bomber pilot in the R.A.F.

Mr. Hough, an enthusiastic follower of auto racing since he was ten years old, covers the sport for a London newspaper. He has also written novels for young racing enthusiasts under his pseudonym, Bruce Carter (see back of jacket for titles).

At present Mr. Hough lives in London with his wife, Charlotte, an artist and book illustrator, and their four children—all girls.

Format by The Etheredges
Set in linotype Scotch
Composed by The Haddon Craftsmen, Inc.
Printed by Murray Printing Company
Bound by The Haddon Craftsmen, Inc.
HARPER & ROW, PUBLISHERS, INCORPORATED